Rita E

MY SOUL IS ....UND

RITA
BORENSTEIN

MY SOUL
IS A
DIAMOND

LET MY TRUE LIGHT SHINE

Rita Borenstein Publishing
2021

Other books by Rita Borenstein Publishing

IN ENGLISH

Rita Borenstein: *To Soul Home and Back – About Life Between Lives*® *hypnotherapy for spiritual regression*, 2018

IN SWEDISH

Rita Borenstein: *Själens resa hem – Möt din själ i livet mellan liven,* 2020
Min själ är en diamant – Låt mitt sanna jag lysa, 2021

Michael Newton: *Själarnas resa – Fallstudier om livet mellan liven,* 2020

ISBN 978-91-986498-1-9

www.ritaborenstein.se

Cover illustration: Mattonstock
Photographs: Peter Bodhi Anand Ullberg, www.bodhi-anand.com
Author photograph: private

Graphic design by Lilla blå tornet, Sweden
www.lillablatornet.se

*Should this my firm persuasion of the soul's
immortality prove to be a mere delusion,
it is at least a pleasing delusion,
and I will cherish it to my last breath.*

Marcus Tullius Cicero 106-43 BC

~

Content

~

To my dear parents,
Rosemarie and Salomon Borenstein.
Thank you for your kindness, support
and love.

~

Foreword

~

By **Dorothea Fuckert M.D.**
July 2020, Germany

Rita Borenstein is an LBL-therapist and author in Sweden. In her second book, she again writes about her work with Life Between Lives® Spiritual Regression. This is a proven hypnotherapy method, developed by the late Dr. Michael Newton. He described it in three bestselling books. About 200 therapists from the Michael Newton Institute (MNI), practicing in about 40 countries around the globe, conducted about 65 000 LBL-sessions altogether according to the MNI research department. Michael Newton alone performed 7 000 sessions from the 1970's on.

In *A Vision of Our Mission* he wrote: *"Our basic goal is to help people move beyond the mindless strife in their physical existence to an inner peace through self-discovery.... The focus of what we do is devoted to the individual seeking answers to the age-old questions of: Who am I, where do I come from, why am I here and where am I going?"*
www.newtoninstitute.org

Rita, also serving as Certification Mentor Coordinator and Director of Membership for MNI, illustrates this therapy brilliantly. It is often just called *Soul Journey* in which clients are facilitated into deep hypnotic trance states and then through specific stations. They can recall pleasant memories in childhood and womb, significant past lives including death, transition and then above all their unique immortal soul in a beautiful world of light, peace and love. Rita exemplifies this single 4-5 hours long session with its transforming impact by three well selected cases, one of them her own personal LBL. There is nothing more authentic and convincing to read from an author than a truthful report of her/his own personal experience. Rita tells the readers about her fourth LBL-session with me as LBL-facilitator. On Easter 2019, we gave each other another great opportunity to explore our souls even deeper, to communicate intensely with our spirit guides and soul friends. In a vivid, comprehensible and appreciative way she describes the wonderful processes of healing, enlightenment and growth which can be brought about by an LBL-session. Some of these were confirmed months later in letters from her clients Ketki and Terry Evans. Their letters are included in the book.

The intent Rita has with *My soul is a diamond – Let my true light shine* is heartfelt and tangible for the reader. It comes with high competence, wisdom and compassion. By this title, she addresses the light of the unique soul or 'true self' of the human being. I prefer to call it the 'great self' compared to the 'small self', usually called the 'false self'. The 'small self' is what we think we are, the 'great self' is what we truly are. The 'small self' is the disconnected personality self with its self-doubts, rumination, anxieties, fears, guilt feelings and shame. The 'ego', a part of the 'small self', always struggling, is the actual 'shadow self', as it makes us the biggest problems with its dualistic thinking, ambition, control, perfectionism, fault-finding, envy, greed, illusions, inflations and egocentrism. The 'great self' or soul is the magnificent divine essence which is always connected to all that is. Current natural sciences, based on materialistic-mechanistic paradigms, don't want to recognize a thousand years old knowledge: The physical human body with its chemistry, biology and genetics is centered within the pervading and surrounding energy field of the soul. The currently valid worldview decides on the question if there is a soul or not. For most of its times of existence humankind assumed one.

The soul is a conscious, immortal, multidimensional energy field, created from a divine intelligent source (called God). She is ample, perennial, resting in herself, yet connected to nature, other beings, the universe and everything. A unique divine spark, our most precious treasure, gifted with special talents. We are incarnating again and again into a physical body in this material, dualistic world to learn, grow and complete ourselves towards a whole 'image of God'. Therefore, we choose an individual life purpose which we want to fulfill during the incarnation. In this developmental way, we are accompanied and supported by personal spirit guides and helpers. After each physical incarnation, we are returning as souls into 'the beyond'. Even nowadays, most humans believe in a soul as well as in an afterlife. Although Christians don't believe in a life before life, they believe in an existence beyond death, called heaven. From MNI's collected 65 000 LBL-sessions (and many near death-experiences worldwide) we know something of this realm. It appears as an eternal dimension, a subtle, limitless and luminous world of light, peace, love, freedom and expanded consciousness. We exist there as souls in affinity to our spirit guides and helpers, to a group of soul friends and in unity with the universe. It is a sphere of recovery, healing, joy, amusement, play, creativity, exploration and more.

There is a point that heaven, angels and God must exist because presumably all humans yearn for it, be it consciously or subconsciously. I found this statement intriguingly simple and logical. We can only yearn for something which we already experienced. This counts for safety, love, trust, joy and basically for every experience. If there wouldn't be an afterlife in another dimension, we wouldn't be able to yearn for it. Each person may decide deliberately to allow for this yearning inside, to believe in a higher intelligent order with a purposeful creation and evolution. This decision informs the sense of life, as deep desire, intent and faith are the most powerful virtues for co-creation.

The question is how people can remember and then live their soul when the ruling principle in the present age is the ubiquitous "I think therefore I am" (René Descartes' "cogito ergo sum"), when the outside, the social façade, is generally more important than the inside. Children in school learn conventional, limited knowledge. While they grow physically into adulthood they shrink into their 'small self'. This is happening by the need to adapt to the rules of a culture with a materialistic-mechanistic world view. In this process, nearly all children must disguise their 'great self', deny their intuitions, suppress their feelings, hold their breath, stiffen their muscles or dissociate with going out of their body. To survive and protect themselves, they need this 'armoring' against their core which means to twist and bend to a secondary form of being. Children at school and students at universities learn that the human being is a sum of its physical biochemistry and that consciousness is only produced by its brain. They must believe that all life is an accidental product which ends at death. They cannot but forget how they as young children still remembered where they came from and who they are.

Until the age of three or four many, not all, children are able to stay in their soul state. It means they maintain their inborn grace, openness and emotional freedom to experience countless moments of joy, spontaneity, sense of trust, unity, curiosity and creativity. Most cultures suppress this 'divine self' through education. Especially western societies denied the soul almost completely from the time of Enlightenment. We are living in a seemingly soulless world, with soulless sciences, medicine, education, agriculture, jobs, economy, commerce, politics and institutions. Only the religions go on to talk about soul and spirit. Yet, this belief is at least in Christians accompanied by putting the divine essence of humans down, especially when it comes to autonomy, pleasure, body and sexuality. In contrast to this widespread negative attitude, recalling and perceiving one's soul in LBL leads to an inner certainty that she brings transcendent goodness, truthfulness and beauty into an imminently good, truthful, beautiful body. Both are divine creations.

The Christian theologian Matthew Fox, one of the extraordinary positive examples, said once in a dialogue with Rupert Sheldrake:[1] *"We suffer from [...] pusillanimity [...] whereas we are all here from magnanimity. We are here to become a great soul, magna anima. [...] All of them* (the mystics, D.F.) *say the same thing: the soul is not in the body, but the body is in the soul. [...] Believing that our body is in our soul means our souls are as large as the world in which we live, as the fields in which our minds play, and as the field in which our hearts roam. That's how big our souls are [...] Magnanimity is not about will-power (I'm going to be a big soul today), it's about following our passions and guiding them to the directions that we're called to go into [...] The mystics are artists of the soul. They are poets of the soul [...] The soul is seen as an expression of a person's total state of being alive* (in Jewish theology, D.F.). *The soul is a totality filled with power. This power lets the soul grow and prosper so it can maintain itself and do its work in the world [...] The important thing is that everybody is absolutely unique [...] However we wander into one another's soul, the home-base, the body which is unique. We should rise and praise when we talk about what friendship is and love is and about what lovers are about – this interpenetration of one another's souls by way of the body. That's so marvelous! I think that angels are envious of humans because we have bodies; they don't, and love-making makes the angels flap their wings in envy [...] That's what the Song of*

Songs is in the Bible. Human sexuality is a mystical moment in the history of the Universe".

In this context, I also think of Marianne Williamson's most popular quote:[2] *"Our deepest fear is that we are powerful beyond measure. It is our light, not our darkness, that most frightens us".*

The 'thick veil' of forgetting, denying and combating is usually causing an awful lot of suffering and misery. Nevertheless, it seems to be an essential part of the soul's overall evolutionary plan. It leads eventually to a recalling of the 'great self' and of its vast resources. However, as in our culture there are no authentic rituals for spiritual self-discovery, soul initiation or ignition of the divine spark, as indigenous people might have had. People need to find new pathways and life-experience to reconnect to their soul and the spirit realm. Thereby, they come to realize that neither religions, churches nor psycho-therapy methods are offering those. Nowadays ever more people search for authentic spirituality, long to find their true self, their soul and fulfill their chosen life purpose, often accompanied by a heartfelt desire to serve humanity and nature and the unconscious intent to integrate divine aspects into the human being.

Dr. Newton's spiritual regression (LBL) is a safe, highly effective and economic method to recall and reconnect to the soul and spirit realms.

In this book, Rita shares her recalling of a meaningful past life as a woman called Leyla. It was a happy, abundant, fulfilled life in which she obviously lived her 'great self'. She describes how she made contact in deep trance with her wise, loving primary guide Alfred. He made it clear to be always with her as friend and mediator between the worlds, as healer by providing safety and support. We anchored this bond as a most helpful resource. After she questions how she could overcome an old residual anxiety, she sees symbolically a crack at the right side of her heart from an old friction, caused by many lonely lives. After Alfred calls in a group of spirit specialists they perform an "open heart surgery", remove the thorns and fix the crack. He confirms that recalling her life as Leyla was essential, because she had lived it with her heart whole and complete and in female grace. The current calling of her soul, he says, is to shift her familiar inner healer more to become a teacher, to express her soul through writing and just to "be still and know". The anxiety had held her 'great self' back for a long time. Meanwhile, it functioned as a reminder of this and as a green light for renewed joy and female grace. I have been in contact with Rita since this session and could witness her wonderful personal growth. It appeared to me like a fine-tuning of her 'divine jewel'. Her soul light is shining anew and bright like a diamond.

Ketki's case story is a parade example for the necessary liberation from a 'small self' or 'false self' which was conditioned in childhood and adolescence to fulfill their parental needs and expectations, adapt to the usual societal standards and follow cultural ideals. The LBL-session with Rita conveyed a deep understanding of herself and her soul's path. She confirmed this in her letters included in the book. The healing key seemed to be her growing into ever more independence, authenticity, outer and inner freedom, self-allowance to listen to her soul's voice, discover her great self and to expand it into the world. As she was still relatively young, she didn't fully experience what is possible in an LBL-session. Something was held back from her, she realized. Yet, she always can receive "assurance and positive thoughts" from a spiritual source, as she wrote later. Her life purpose, after being freed from guilt feelings and shame, is about consciousness, power and love within communities, also about developing a new, wholesome female identity. She revealed brilliance, courage, strength and wisdom, which has, as I intuit, still to sink more from the mind into heart and body.

Terry Evans, a known spiritual medium and teacher in Sweden, is a mature, wise soul, and closely connected to his primary guide since a young age. In the session, he recalled two fascinating past lives. The healing impact of his LBL-experience seemed to be on understanding even deeper why humans are so often cruel and violent, on forgiving, letting go and making peace. The session enabled a transformation of an underlying deep sadness and resignation into new hope and joy, optimism and strength. His soul wishes to manifest his wonderful gifts in service for humanity to the fullest. As clairvoyant, he can see the beauty of an incarnated soul, the light and dark sides.

All three, Rita, Ketki and Terry recalled and integrally healed at least one significant past life, experienced the easy crossing over into their 'Soul Home', this beautiful realm of spirit, a place of learning and reunion. Through intense conversations with guides, soul friends and other wise beings, they got essential life questions answered, while receiving their unconditional acceptance, support, wisdom, humor and love.

With her second book about LBL, Rita Borenstein continues to follow Michael Newton's 'Vision of our Mission':

"Much that divides us spiritually would be further diminished by the knowledge that we all come from the same spiritual sphere and will return at the end of our lives to the same universal place of origin, regardless of who we are, where we live and what we do. A belief that a divine power greater than ourselves exists, without human disciples, but with personal spirit guides, would bring greater harmony to society. The healing of everyone that experiences a spiritual frame-

work of loving order will help others whom they touch in society. In this way, our message will expand by the work we do.

Our organization is pledged to offer a new way with enlightenment springing from the mind of everyone regardless of their prior institutional belief system or lack of it. In the complex world of our present century, people need the conviction more than ever that a divine universal consciousness exists within a pure spiritual order. They must discover this principle within their own minds for real conviction to take place. Eventually, if enough people come to this realization through our efforts, there will hopefully be a lessening of external conflict in our struggle for survival. The ethical compass of humanity would have a stronger meaning since it would come from personal enlightenment. The Michael Newton Institute teaches that the core purpose of souls who come to earth in their incarnations is to bring love, compassion and understanding to others who cross their lives. This moral imperative is blended into our personal karmic purpose to improve life on earth by our being here. Defining individual identity through our hypnosis methodology helps people advance the level of their own energy. The realization of our universal divinity as united souls on earth, each with a conscious knowledge of Self and purpose, would allow for a more positive destiny in our future on this planet".

The book's title *My soul is a diamond – Let my true light shine* is a healing suggestion. Of course, Rita doesn't aim for herself or for her clients to become superhuman, but to live life fully, with whole heart, body, mind and soul, depth and intensity. This means to recognize, accept and integrate the dualities which always exist in oneself and on Earth: spiritual and physical, in- and outside, strength and imperfection, love and fear, pleasure and suffering, good and evil, light and shadow, ascent and descent. Not 'whether or', but 'as well as', a 'reconciling third' (term by Richard Rohr) is for all great spiritual masters the necessary way of healing and evolving towards unconditional love, non-dual consciousness, wisdom and bliss. If the focus would lie predominantly on light or on darkness, half of creation would be denied. That is certainly not what our soul aims for, yet it often happens due to unconscious patterns of avoiding pain and conflict. We should be aware along our path of not to fall again into this very old dualistic trap.

LBL has a pronounced non-directive style as we open to our clients and us as facilitators to receive guidance from our spirit sources. In fact, Rita is a true master in leading her clients subtly, yet clearly and firmly from station to station along this journey till they arrive at the LBL state of their soul, without imposing herself upon them. Her pure intent, kindness and love for people really touches me. Therefore, it was again a great honor and pleasure to write a foreword. I am fully convinced that many people will be attracted to this book. It will generate soul resonance in the reader which will then radiate into the world.

[1] Sheldrake R./Fox, M. *Natural Grace: Dialogues on Science and Spirituality.* Bloomsbury, 1996, 73 ff.
[2] Williamson, M. *Return to Love: Reflections on the Principles of a Course in Miracles.* HarperCollins, 1992, 190 ff.

~

Foreword

~

By **Roger Gotthardsson**
May 2020, Sweden

As everything in life and beyond, I stumbled into Rita's space with what seemed like unlikely coincidences. But with some perspective it all makes perfectly sense. Rarely, or may I even say never, have I met someone that looks so much like me on the inside and so little on the outside. Me – a hard core IT security specialist, Rita – a hypnotherapist working with Life Between Lives spiritual regressions. We may use different methods, metaphors and words, but we are both travelers into spaces unknown to shallow consciousness in this century. Spaces we seem to have forgotten, but somehow deeply familiar to us, once we scratch the surface of our awareness.

I came across the Michael Newton Institute via Michael's books some years ago. I can't recall exactly how, but as with most things I am sure I got some help. For many years I have followed the Robert Monroe Institute and their modelling of consciousness. The two organizations are describing the same phenomena with different words and angles, but stunningly coherent. The Newton approach is through guidance from a therapist, while Monroe is using guided soundwaves to boost your meditation states. Being highly visual, the areas described as Life Between Lives-state is analogous with what the Monroe institute calls Focus 27. This is the state where souls who departed earth gather at reunion. The place is joyful, very healing and you may explore new skills. In the Newton LBL-sessions Rita facilitates you often also experience your previous incarnations. This is a very strong method to heal current life and to avoid unwanted karmic repetition. A pure perspective on karmic lesions can be a gigantic leap forward in personal development.

Let me reveal the secret about hypnotherapy: The old belief that the hypnotherapist has secret tricks to make you sleep, is totally wrong. It is quite the opposite; the therapist is an experienced traveler into altered states of consciousness. She/he will awaken you to these states, sometimes by slightly dimming down your current perceptions via hypnosis or meditation. Your hypnotherapist cannot guide anyone anywhere without going there her/himself. The secret is that the therapist is very good at changing mental states and maintaining control and awareness. Deep empathy is also a requirement to experience what another person is experiencing in real time and in altered mental states. This is empathy beyond our regular sensory input reflection from the physical plane. If you intend to travel into unknown places my recommendation is to bring the most experienced guide you can find. But don't just be a boring tourist riding the bus and force-feed altered state information. Instead: Participate, interact, explore, inspire, learn, create, help, try new things so your experiences can be a natural part of our new reality. I believe this is how our species can evolve and grow.

The skills Rita has developed over the years is to maintain the state of being consciously aware in LBL/F27 and at the same time being aware in this reality frame. She has developed and refined the skills of inner travelling with full awareness. The skills Rita has developed are amazing, but a totally natural evolution of an old experienced soul. Being aware that you have been dreaming, or actually – are dreaming – is what we call awakening. In a full awakened state, we are aware that the separation from source we are often painfully experiencing – the disconnect – is only a belief we carried for a while. Rita is helping so many people to get a glimpse of the realities beyond.

So, thank you Rita, for your guidance and helping us to wake up.

PART 1

~

Introduktion

~

I thought of the soul as resembling a castle
formed of a single diamond
or a very transparent crystal.
Containing many rooms, just
as in Heaven there are many mansions.

Teresa of Avila

in her book "The interior castle" published in 1588

Introduction

My true calling

Know all the theories, master all the techniques,
but as you touch a human soul,
be just another human soul.

C.G. JUNG

I worked many years as a nurse before I finally gave in to my true calling. To research the beauty and wisdom of the human soul is what I enjoy the most. In 2012, I trained with the Michael Newton Institute (MNI) and became the first Life Between Lives®(LBL)-facilitator in Sweden. In the company of 200 fellow global members I carry on the legacy and life work of Dr. Michael Newton. Dr. Newton is the author of three best-selling books, *Journey of Souls: Case Studies of Life Between Lives, Destiny of Souls: New Case Studies of Life Between Lives* and *Life Between Lives: Hypnotherapy for Spiritual Regression.*

Dr. Newton had an international reputation as a spiritual

regressionist who mapped out much of our experience as souls. He appeared on numerous radio and TV-talk shows to explain our immortal life in the spirit world.

The Newton Institute was established in 2005 by him and a group of pioneers he trained. His legacy after he retired in 2006 and died in 2016 is carried on by our members and led by a Board of Directors. The name of our organization is now the Michael Newton Institute. MNI is the foremost organization of Life Between Lives® research. The institute provides training seminars to professional audiences around the world and has also published many books.

On our website, *www.newtoninstitute.org*, you will find an online journal called *Stories of the Afterlife*. It includes new LBL-case stories and interesting articles about our work.

Over the years, I have facilitated a lot of sessions here in Sweden. My intention was not primarily to write books about it, but it has become a personal challenge to try to document the essence of what I learned and experienced in my work with this method.

In September 2018, I published my first book *To Soul Home and Back – about Life Between Lives hypnotherapy for spiritual regression.* It was a very fulfilling experience to become a publisher of my own book. I was truly surprised and delighted that so many readers booked their own LBL-session with me after they read my book.

The theme of my second book *My soul is a diamond – Let my true light shine* is about coming out as a soul and to fulfill my deepest desire to shine bright and clear in this life. To shine bright does not mean that I idealize myself or that I am in a happy mood all day long. Of course, I have my ups and downs in life. For me, shining bright means to be in touch with my soul and to become myself as a human being, as much as possible. As soon as I decided to go ahead with the new book project, I scheduled my fourth LBL with my dear MNI colleague Dr. Dorothea Fuckert in Germany. The trip to Dorothea in April 2019 was very special to me. Not only did I enjoy spending time with her, but we also gave each other the gift of facilitating sessions for each other. It was a profound and deeply healing experience.

This book includes dialogues from my session facilitated by Dorothea and my reflections about the impact it had on my life. I also present two LBL-client case stories with dialogues and comments. One of the stories is about the adorable Ketki and the chapter is called "Contentment". The other one is about Terry Evans who is a famous clairvoyant here in Sweden. I named the chapter about him The importance of purposeful friends. Both Ketki and Terry Evans have been ever so kind to me with letters and comments about their sessions. Their letters are included in the book.

Like with many other events in my life one thing led to the

other and suddenly I became a book publisher, without really knowing how it happened. I enjoy being open to where my inner compass is leading me. When I was younger I literally threw my hat over the wall and then made a huge leapfrog to go after it. I was constantly taking leaps of faith and sometimes I ended up in disaster. But I always learned something. Growing older and hopefully with more experience I prefer not to make hasty decisions, but to rather be easy on myself and to do what I enjoy in a more self-caring and down to earth manner. I am also a gardener who loves all aspects from seed to flower and the changes of seasons.

PART 2

~

Nurture and cherish
the soul

~

*Rita, imagine that there is a beautiful butterfly
sitting on your shoe. When the wings move,
take it as a sign of green light for action.
If the wings are still, just wait, do nothing.
And always remember to breathe!*

THE WISDOM OF MY DEAR LIFE-MENTOR G.S.

Nurture and cherish
the soul

I love my life

I am sitting in the shade under a wonderful and lush tree. It is overflowing with delicious and fresh peaches. The weather is warm and pleasant. I can hear a soft pouring sound from a water fountain and it makes me feel so peaceful. My dress is loosely draped around me and the colors and textures of my clothes give me a sense of grace and beauty. Sitting here under the peach tree brings back memories from my life.

My name is Leyla. I came to this palace as a young girl. My parents brought me here when it was time to marry my beloved husband whom they had chosen for me. He was also young and shy. I did not know how to be a woman then, but slowly and with time we learned to know each other. I love him deeply. And I love my life. I am so happy!

My faith is strong. My husband and I were meant to be together. Slowly my love for him grew stronger. I learned from him about life. In his presence and compassion for me I knew myself better. We are blessed with many children and grand-children. Now I am old, wise and deeply content. My life has been overflowing with happiness, soulful beauty, faith and richness with a loving and wonderful partner, many healthy and strong children, a large family and dear close friends. My days and life passed by inside the walls of this palace. This is the paradise on earth that I know. I am so fond of it. It is my home. There was no need to travel anywhere, because all I ever wanted, I had here. We have plenty of food and riches. There is peace in our country. My husband inherited the palace when his father died. Since I first met him I have been by his side. He loves me beyond measure. And I love him.

We often have large and festive gatherings here in the palace. Then I always wear my most beautiful dress in many different colors and jewels chosen for each occasion. My hair has always been long and it feels so nice with many pins and different styles. My husband and I support and feel much respect for each other. For me the most important thing is to be here and enjoy my life in the palace. There are people who take care of all the practical things, so after I gave birth to our children, all I did was to be with them and enjoy being their mother. We have a friendly atmosphere here. It is a harmonious and serene place. I sometimes go to one of my favorite spots here in the palace garden where I have a view over the hills outside the walls. From where I am now sitting, I can see the sky, the sun, the clouds and the world outside our palace which is on a hill. Oh, how wonderful my life is! At night, I can see all the stars.

My LBL-session with Dorothea

In April 2019, I travelled to Germany and had my fourth LBL with Dr. Dorothea Fuckert. Dorothea is an LBL-facilitator and M.D., psychotherapist and author. She embodies a rich personal and professional source of wisdom and knowledge. So, to say the least, I was in good hands. In the LBL I experienced a perfectly happy past life as a woman called Leyla. My speculation after the session is that Leyla might have lived in Seville when the city was called Taífa Ishbiliya in al-Andalus (Muslim Spain) in the period AD 712-1248.

In my session, deeply hypnotized, I also experienced myself dying after choking from a peach seed was stuck in my throat. In the moment of crossing over I was looking down on the people in the castle trying to resuscitate me on the floor, but I was already on my way to soul home again. My beloved husband had died earlier and I was happy to follow him. In my incarnation as Leyla I had an authentic and strong faith, which was very healing for me to experience as Rita. Leyla believed in a higher power and had no worries or doubts about anything. When Dorothea asked how I felt about my own death as Leyla, I responded calmly: "It was such a happy life. Now I will return home."

A crack in my heart

The wound is the place where The Light enters you.

RUMI

One of the questions for my session with Dorothea was how to heal my anxiety. I wanted to get to the bones of why I had periods of anxiety during the past seven years. What was this kind of suffering showing me from my soul perspective? What did I learn from the experience? What could heal the anxiety? How could I help myself in all of this? I had many questions!

Dorothea had a wonderful way to help me connect with my soul and spiritual guidance for further help to understand the reasons. This is a dialogue taking place in the beginning of the LBL when I was gradually going into an altered hypnotic state of relaxation.

Rita: *I can see a picture of a heart!*

Dorothea: Anything else you feel there? The heart can hold many feelings at the same time.

R: *I can see a symbol of a heart. On the right side of the heart there is a small crack. There is a small piece missing!*

D: As if a small piece is missing there. Aha, that is very interesting. It will be helpful when we come back to this later in our journey. All right? We could ask your guides what it is. The cause for it and how it can heal completely. Just breathe into it now and let it be.

R: *The picture is changing now and the heart symbol turns, so I can see it from the right side. Now I can see the details! I realize that the heart is very old. The missing piece on the right side is from a long, long time of friction. A piece has not been ripped off, but the friction was created over time. Then the crack was created and a piece fell off. It is a very clear picture!*

D: It is an important picture for you obviously. It is helpful that you see it so clearly. We will come back to this later in our communication with your guides. We will come back to the heart! Okay? To this crack specially! Let the feelings be. Let them come and go with the breathing. Diving deeper in the now. That's right. I want you to imagine yourself in some place where you feel very, very safe and calm, relaxed, protected and connected. Any way you would like to feel now?

In the beginning of my session and with the soothing voice of Dorothea, I experienced a sensation which I felt as "a piece missing in my heart". You will notice by reading the dialogues with me deeply hypnotized, that I will find the missing peace, not only in my heart, but metaphorically in my life as Rita in general.

The dialogue with Dorothea shows that she acts like "an advocate" for my soul. She pays attention to what I'm saying about the crack in my heart, but she suggests we save it for later in the session, when I go deeper into an altered state of relaxation and meet my spirit guides and support team.

Dorothea stayed by my side as the skilled LBL-facilitator she is and this way helped me feel safe, grounded and deeply relaxed through the whole session. She told me to go to "a safe place". This is a hypnotherapy technique called "a deepener". For the client deeply hypnotized there is no conception of time and place. By asking me "to go to some place where you feel very, very safe and calm", Dorothea helped me have a sense of being totally safe like a newborn in the arms of a loving mother. This helped me go deeper into an altered state of deep relaxation. Feeling very safe it was possible to access the levels of awareness where spiritual guides, higher beings and deceased loved ones are there to help and assist my soul travelling in the inner journey. This way the session gradually becomes a team work with the spirit world. The deeper the client goes, the more it is possible to access soul memories. This was one of the great findings in the research done by Dr. Newton and by members of MNI.

LBL versus near death-experience (NDE)

For those who conclude reincarnation is the truth, the obvious fact still is that we live each life only once. It is, at least for me, very challenging when I think of one day having to say goodbye to my life, loved ones and to this world.

I met a few people who had a near death-experience (NDE) and afterwards could explain to others how it felt to die. Dr. Eben Alexander wrote three books about his experience from his NDE. He was in a coma for a week and then came back and recovered. He explains his experience in his two books *Proof of heaven* and *The map of heaven.* Being a neurosurgeon he was also able to share his knowledge from a physiological perspective, which made his story even more fascinating. In his third book *Living in a mindful Universe,* which he wrote with Karen Newell, he shares his experience from his own LBL, as well. One could say that an LBL is a way to have an NDE without risking one's life, as is often the case with NDE which happens "by accident" like for example during cardiac arrest.

The whole point with exploring past life and life between lives is to help clients make the best out of their present life and situation. It is also a way to take off the life pressure and to have a bigger picture from their soul perspective. For many of my clients who fear death, this is a way of "going to heaven without dying". Then they know from their own experience what it is like to die. Many of them told me that death seemed less scary after their LBL-experience.

In the following dialogue, Dorothea is guiding me with questions about my death in my past life as Leyla. I met someone after crossing over to the spirit world. This someone is helping me to go through a kind of cleansing which Michael Newton called "the healing shower". After a lifetime and before returning to the afterlife many of my clients tell me about this kind of cleansing of the soul. It is like taking a shower after a day of hard work. In my case the one helping me was a very feminine character resembling a nun and dressed in white. She used a brush to cleanse away "the dust" from my soul after my life as Leyla. I was very moved and thankful for the help I received.

Dorothea: Was your death unexpected?

Rita: *Yes. I was enjoying a delicious peach. Suddenly, the seed was stuck in my throat and I died. But I knew it was meant to be this way.*

D: Aha, but now you are a free soul.

R: *I've come to this place now, where I can connect.*

D: Right!

R: *Here there are souls who move around softly and dressed in white and they take care of me. They have all sorts of devices and they work with sound. They put me on a kind of couch. One of them has a brush. She takes away layers of "dust". They don't say anything. They just do what they do.*

D: Okay. Fascinating!

R: *On my left side is a character resembling a nun. She is taking care of me. She totally knows what to do. The others are busy. I think they are busy with others. It is her job to check me after my death. I came here quite fast and she took me away ... she prepared me.*

D: Oh, she prepares you?

R: *Yes!*

D: How fascinating.

R: *Yes. I am in good hands.*

D: You trust them. You know you are in good hands.

R: *I feel free, because I don't have a body.*

D: Yes, you can expand.

R: *I am so amazed that she is doing this to me. It was such a fulfilling life. It was 100% fulfillment.*

D: Yes, it was.

R: *I am totally amazed.*

D: Yes, maybe it was the most fulfilling life you ever had on earth.

R: *Yes, in the life of Leyla I can feel my total essence as a soul.*

The primary soul guide

As LBL-facilitator my mission is to advocate a relaxation deep enough for my client to enter a receptive state. This condition makes it possible to meet with their own soul and personal guide. Dr. Newton found in his work with 7 000 clients that we all have, what he called, a primary soul guide. His findings were that souls have many secondary soul guides as well, but only one primary guide who is the most important guide for the soul. Several primary guides sometimes take turns to assist the soul through eons of time. During an LBL it is essential that the client meets the primary soul guide, because it is the guide, not me, who is guiding the client through the experience. After the client meets the guide I will ask questions like: "Where does your guide want to take you now?" "Let's ask your guide for the answer to your questions now!"

Here is a dialogue showing how meeting with my primary soul guide happened. After the client connects with the primary guide during the LBL their close relationship will deepen and continue as a possibility for the client after the session.

Some clients already have a close connection with their primary guide before their LBL.

Dorothea: Connect now with your guide! I would like to ask your primary guide to come forward. You may remember him or her as clearly as possible. Reconnect with him! Renew this bond with him! I don't know if it's a he or a she.

Rita: *It's a male. He stands in front of me now.*

D: Come closer, dear guide! Come closer to your protégé, so she can perceive you as clearly as possible.

R: *He feels like a father figure in a monastery. The hat and dress are all in black.*

D: And what is he radiating? Feel his radiation now and tell me!

R: *He is radiating old wisdom. He has short grey hair. He wears a small black simple hat. I can see his eyes. He has warm brown eyes.*

D: Look into his eyes. What are his eyes expressing?

R: *Love and understanding.*

D: Feel this love coming to you. He wants to fulfill his love, his understanding, his warmth. Now, let yourself be filled up with it. It streams into you, through you and around you. He envelopes you and he bathes you in his love and under-standing.

R: *He is coming towards me now. He is draping something like a cape around me, so that I can sense my soul character more.*

D: Okay, so now sense your soul character more.

R: *I am quite a serious character as a soul. He wants to take me to a library. It is Gothic style. He is walking with me very closely and he says: "I will show you something!" It is a feeling of being in a monastery or something like that. Now we go straight ahead into a kind of huge hall, which is like a library. He walks close to me, because he needs to take me there. I am not alone at all!*

D: He is with you!

R: *Now we are here inside.*

D: Do you feel that he is your primary guide?

R: *Yes!*

D: Dear guide, what is your name?

R: *His name is Alfred!*

D: Alfred, since when are you this soul's primary guide?

R: *Since the time when my soul started to develop more into what it is now. He came when I had a life in a monastery where I could not stand it anymore.*

D: I see! And what is your main purpose for Rita's soul, Alfred? What kind of guidance is your specialty?

R: *It is wisdom. Mostly alchemy. It is an original wisdom in a sense.*

Although I had experienced meeting guides and other higher beings in my three LBL-sessions before, this time I had the most intense feeling of connecting with Alfred. It was a great relief to feel the wisdom and love he radiated. I felt very safe when he came to me so clearly. From then on, I consider him my dear friend and mediator between his reality and mine.

Afterlife and loving support

After the death moment in my past life as Leyla and meeting with Alfred, my journey as a soul in the afterlife continued in the following dialogue. Dorothea facilitates by asking my guide where he wants to take me further.

Dorothea: Alfred, what would you like to show your protégé now?

Rita: *Alfred is holding on to me very tightly and we go to the first stop in the building. This is like a cathedral in a sense, but it is also a library. There are no books here. It is more like an altar. I don't know what it is. We are just standing here by a place which feels like an altar and looks like a balcony, but it is not a balcony.*

D: The details are not so important. Try to grasp the essence.

R: *I am holding onto a rail in front of me. Then I remember something. I look at Alfred and ask him now: "What is it that I remember?"*

D: What is his answer?

R: *He tells me that I can remember my support now.*

D: Okay, feel the support!

R: *I am holding on to this rail and I feel the support from Alfred on my left side.*

D: We anchor this support by him and the energy you get from your left side. What is it with this rail that you hold on to? What does it mean to you? What is it that your soul tries to remember or reactivate?

R: *I am asking Alfred now!*

D: Yes, please.

R: *He says that I need to remember that I am supported.*

D: Now, take this knowledge into your heart center and into the depth of your soul. You are supported! Dear Alfred, how can Rita establish a day to day contact and communication with you in her earthly life?

R: *He says: "I will be with her."*

D: Where in her body can she feel your bonding and your connectedness with her, Alfred?

R: *In her stomach.*

D: Thank you, feel your connectedness with Alfred! That's very helpful, Alfred, thank you. Would you like me to ask Alfred your questions now?

R: *Yes!*

D: Dear Alfred, thank you very much for being close now, so that Rita can perceive you clearly and feel your energies and receive your messages and information.

Deep healing

I am sorry.
Please forgive me.
Thank you.
I love you.

THE HO'OPONOPONO PRAYER

In an LBL the important and existential questions the client brings to the session can be answered by the client's soul and primary guide or wise beings who seem to have an interest in the development of this individual soul. Before every session, I ask the client to send me a list of their most important questions. These are the questions we explore and hopefully receive answers to during the session. Sometimes the guides seem to offer and perform healing in certain moments in the session. When this happens the room where I am sitting with my client is filled with stillness, serenity, warmth and love. I just lean back in my chair quietly and close my eyes to enjoy the moment fully with my client when the spiritual healing team seems to be at work. With Dorothea, I had the opportunity to feel a kind of spiritual "heart surgery". Here is the dialogue with Dorothea while it happens.

Rita: *Wait a moment, I think Alfred does something to me now. I think he prepares me.*

Dorothea: He prepares you?

R: *Yes, because I could feel a short anxiety like he was showing me the anxiety Rita had for so long. He says I need some time to work with Rita's body before the questions are asked. He is healing me!*

D: Good!

R: *He does things to me. It feels very good.*

D: What is he doing? Can you describe it?

R: *He does something to my heart. He is taking away the thorns. He says it is like an open-heart surgery. In the beginning, I felt symptoms which I recognized as the unpleasant sensations of anxiety. It is like a surgical intervention taking place now. He does something to the heart and he calls in some "specialists" as well. They are working on the crack. They fix the crack!*

D: Yes, you are grateful that they fixed the crack now. Shall I ask what the cause was for this crack? Alfred, what was the primary cause for and what caused this crack?

R: *It has to do with her present life, but also other lives she had as a soul.*

D: And what was the primary experience when this crack started?

R: *Her soul experienced many lonely lives. But somehow, she could feel support from the spirit world in the darkest moments. The life of Leyla is so important to remember, because then she was complete and whole. So, this is what they are going to fix, to make my heart whole again.*

D: Thank you very much, Alfred.

R: *He says that he calls in some other helpers. There is a whole group working with me now. It feels very nice! I feel the support.*

D: Amazing! You are safe and you trust.

R: *It is like an open-heart surgery.*

D: Wow! You are safe. Do you feel any anxiety?

R: *No, not at all. But when he started to work on me, I briefly* *felt a longing to go out of my body, but then I realized I am not my body. So, no worries!*

D: You are safe. You are in the best of hands that you can imagine at all.

R: *This feels very good. I am in the hands of specialists.*

D: Feel how good it is.

R: *It feels like they are the best specialists who are helping me now. Alfred too!*

D: Feel the healing take place. You heal now. Your heart, your soul.

R: *As this is happening I feel as if I am lying on a golden couch. All this is happening in perfect order.*

D: Wow! I can imagine.

R: *Alfred says that he has been with me all the time, but Rita could not sense him as closely before.*

D: Now you can perceive him whenever you want.

R: *Yes.*

D: He is always with you. You are never alone. He is always with you.

R: (I cry tears of joy.) *Yes!*

All my questions are answered

The important thing is to recognize our faults,
avoid self-denial, and have the courage
and self-sufficiency to make
constant adjustments in our lives.

MICHAEL NEWTON,

JOURNEY OF SOULS: CASE STUDIES OF LIFE BETWEEN LIVES

After the healing of my heart Dorothea continues to ask Alfred the questions I, as Rita, brought to the session. There is a blissful feeling after the healing was orchestrated so beautifully and my heart magically mended. This helped me relax even deeper.

Dorothea: Is now the moment we could ask the other questions?

Rita: *Yes. The preparation goes on simultaneously, so we can continue with the questions. They still work on me.*

D: Yes, they continue while we speak with Alfred.

R: *They know what to do.*

D: Alfred, how could Rita contact and communicate with her other guides in this current earthly life? For instance, with these surgeons if she needs them.

R: *Alfred says that he is my main and primary guide and has always been. He will call them in, if needed. He says that I don't really need to bother, because they are not connected to me.*

D: Dear Alfred, another question. This crack, which was in the heart center, did it have anything to do with Rita's anxiety?

R: *Yes.*

D: Help us understand, Alfred.

R: *I feel there is something with the incarnation as Leyla and with the choking. Rita's fear is all about dying before she has completed her life.*

D: I understand. That is her basic right. And what could she contribute? How can she heal this anxiety forever, fully? What is the remedy, Alfred?

R: *He says: "I am the remedy!"*

D: There you have it!

R: *Alfred says that he is the remedy! I am so happy.*

D: Because he gives you safety, strength, wisdom and understanding. And love.

R: *He is telling me that in Rita's other relationships and in all relationships, not only the men she has been close to, she makes herself smaller. She puts up with the small crumbs from the bread. She thought that she cannot get what she needs and wants. But everything was of course orchestrated this way for a reason. Now when she is older, her anxiety is kicking in and helping her as a reminder, because now she wants to feel that love and satisfaction again which she felt as Leyla. The small breadcrumbs are not enough to nourish her anymore.*

D: Of course! And Alfred, what was the function of making herself smaller than she was? And the function of this anxiety? What purpose did this anxiety have?

R: *To make her long for herself as much as possible. Her true self.*

D: So, the purpose of your former anxiety and making yourself smaller than you are was to now remember that you long for yourself. Long for your true self and for your soul and all your essences. And that you also may trust yourself. You are lovable! You are love! He reminds you of that. He supports you in this.

R: *Alfred says that it is really a delicate thing for all souls, but for me it is an especially delicate thing, because when I re-incarnated this time, I knew that everything was kind of tricky. I know that I am a healer soul from before. My purpose is to heal myself and help others heal. Now I am somehow on the verge of changing to become more of a teacher's soul.*

D: That sounds convincing to me. More of a teacher. You have access to higher wisdom through your soul. Do I understand it correctly, Alfred, that her soul wants to teach? To be more of a teacher?

R: *Yes, we can call it a step to another level. It is like wearing another hat. Rita is stepping from healer to teacher. She has learned a lot about healing in many incarnations. Now as Rita, she can fast speed the whole thing. Rita needs to get this. I thank Alfred so much for not showing himself to me earlier with this great wisdom, because if he would have come earlier, I would have lost my way.*

My soul is a diamond

The belief system of a "Self" partly
holds its integrity between realities, also through
death. On higher levels in Consciousness,
this is by choice, as an expression. Make your
expression shine, that's your job!

ROGER GOTTHARDSSON

The duration of an LBL spiritual regression usually is 3–5 hours. This is a long time for a person to be deeply hypnotized. My session with Dorothea was 3,5 hours.

After the client crosses over from the death moment in a past life and the journey to soul home starts, the primary guide usually meets the protégé. It is the primary soul guide who takes the soul into a place where the questions the client brought to the session can be asked by the LBL-facilitator, in my case Dorothea. The client will answer from their inner knowing, seeing or hearing what the guide or other beings and helpers answer. So, the soul and the guide and other higher beings speak through the client. The more deeply relaxed a client is, the smaller the risk of bias by the client's ego. This is the most frequent obstacle for an authentic spiritual regression. As a hypnotherapist, I need to be aware of what is called "conscious interference", which means the information might come from the ego of the client rather than from their own soul.

It is also important to prevent what we call "entity confusion". This is not knowing who is saying what, and both the client and I can become confused. We want clarity in questions and answers and for the client to receive answers to the often-asked existential questions brought to the session. Honesty, being precise and very present is the greatest contribution an LBL-facilitator can offer the client. I want to prevent a situation when the clients would leave my practice more confused than when they came.

Dorothea: Dear Alfred, how can Rita shine as brightly as possible?

Rita: *This is by doing her writing and just to be still and live quietly. Rita now lives and works in beautiful surroundings close to nature. That's it. She can just be there and all will come to her.*

D: What is the best way for her to teach?

R: *Alfred and Rita as a team will know what to teach.*

D: I see. You are a spiritual teaching team.

R: *And Alfred is happy now because ... why is he happy? He is smiling.*

D: Yes, because he knew. Alfred, do you have any information for your protégé which could help Rita with her second book about her work?

R: *Alfred will help her in all these things. He knows!*

D: Thank you again, Alfred.

D: The last question on Rita's list is: "Alfred, I'd like to investigate why Rita has become so serious and seldom cracks jokes anymore like she used to. She misses the fun and has become so serious, for some reason. Alfred, please let her understand the reason for the seriousness and the lack of fun and play. Help her reconnect with her joy, if possible."

R: *Alfred says that it was quite an effort from the spirit world to hold Rita back for so many years. The anxiety was part of it and made her more introverted, also helped her pay attention to her heart's desire. She was fighting against it most of the time, because she was so used to acting in an extrovert* *manner. And this holding back from the spirit world has been going on for some time, at least for twenty years. It doesn't matter really, but it has been a long time. It started after her marriage ended and after that she had to become more serious. She had to perceive herself seriously, she had to work with her inner child, she had to do all this to be done with it, in a sense. It does not only have to do with this incarnation. It comes from a lot of incarnations where she, as a soul, has been a healer and collected a lot of information that she can now teach as Rita.*

Rita needs to see the whole picture. With anxiety, she has not seen the whole picture because she had tunnel vision. Many and massive layers of fear and body-armor have blocked her joy. Alfred says that she will not only see with both her eyes. Rita will also see with her third eye. Not all the time, but when needed to see through the illusion.

D: Good to know. Alfred, I would like to come back to the question about the lack of joy and play. I understood as Rita did, that it was necessary to become serious, but is she allowed from now on to have more joy and fun, to become lighter?

R: *Yes, she will feel joy in the moment. Complete joy occasionally.*

D: Alfred, what was the reason for remembering her life as Leyla?

R: *It is about the feminine grace and beauty. During the serious period, Rita did not care about her physicality and looks. She used to love very feminine dresses and jewelry all her life, just like Leyla. This is coming back now and to be more feminine. Maybe grow her hair long again as well.*

D: But your soul does not want that any longer. Your soul wants to live these special qualities. And you have a social function with this somehow. Your books, talks and conferences and whatever you will create. And you will shine bright like a diamond.

A reflection a year after my LBL

My session and meeting with Dorothea helped me understand and remember that I am loved and supported, which is easy to forget in times of isolation, challenges, anxiety and depression. Remembering my past life as Leyla and meeting my primary guide Alfred clearly and thoroughly had a very healing effect on me. Feeling supported and deeply understood and mirrored both by the spirit world and by a loving human being like Dorothea, was very important to me. I have realized that my anxiety helped me become aware of my old wounds and to mend them one by one, deeper and deeper. It helped me grow as a woman, healer and teacher.

When I meet clients, write books and articles, give public talks and workshops, I experience a great inner joy in fulfilling my life's purpose. It takes time and much awareness to heal like an onion from inside out, from the top to the bottom and layer by layer. My life experience helped me practice the art of patience and acceptance. Also, forgiveness of myself and others is an important factor in my healing.

Thank you, dear Doro, my LBL-colleague and dear soul sister, for your wonderful and loving way to support me and my soul to "come out" and shine in this life.

PART 3

~

Contentment

~

The contentment.
It is not about fame or power.
It is like growing tomatoes in your own garden.

KETKI

I love going to school

My name is Ketki and I am twelve years old. I like to sit in class and listen to the lectures and pay attention. I don't like doing my homework. I try to maintain things, as I don't like to get a remark in my calendar. I don't like to overdo it either. I do well in exams. My teachers are happy. My parents are happy with me! There is a lot of pressure, because dad wants me to be top of the class and not just one of the good students. Especially when it comes to mathematics, he wants me to score full marks. Sometimes I worry that I would come second or even third and that would not be taken nicely. Overall I am happy. After school, there are tennis lessons. My tennis coach is very nice and friendly. He understands us very well and we have a good time. My sister and I have a lot of video games in our room. We have our own TV and many video cassettes, and we watch cartoons and movies. Sometimes I feel that if I had more time to focus on studying, I would not be so exhausted with the homework, because there is always tennis after school. I like playing with my coach and with my sister, but I am not competitive by nature. I don't really enjoy participating in tournaments, but dad really wishes that we do well. My sister is very competitive. She has high spirit and she completely enjoys it. I just go, because I have a really good time there. But then when I am back, I have no energy left to do anything. Then I just want to relax.

I don't like that we don't get to attend birthday parties or go for sleepovers, because we would miss tennis lessons. We even miss our own birthday parties, because dad doesn't let us skip tennis lessons, even for our own birthday party. Everybody is kind of waiting and dad rushes us and makes sure we play tennis and then we go home. Dad thinks that if we work hard now, we have a chance to become professional players. I think it is too stressful for me to be in a competitive environment. I would rather not be in that sort of thing. I am a little chubby and overweight and that worries me. My father calls me those things publicly, many times. He discusses my weight with my coach and other people. I don't like it! This makes me cry telling you about it. I feel so humiliated when he does this to me. I have low self-confidence and feel insecure. My sister is very athletic and fit. She scores high marks easily. She does well.

My mum thinks education is very important, because her family and parents were not educated. She thinks that her husband is very educated and therefore her daughters have a better chance for the future. She had a hard time convincing her *parents to let her graduate and now she is in the house, not even able to work. She thinks that even though it is hard for her daughter now, I will do well in the future. She just wants her daughters to have more possibilities in life than she had.*

It is truly a lot of pressure. Not only to make dad happy, but also mum. I know how much is at stake for her. She really, really wants the best for her children. She thought the best way she could have was marrying someone who is really educated, ambitious and into sports. Someone who will give her opportunities for her kids that she herself could not get. That is why she truly believed that this will lead to a good future. She was not thinking about her own happiness or whether she was getting anything out of the marriage.

Dad had this thing that you had to manage time every day. Just because there is an exam coming up, you cannot miss your tennis class. So, there is no leeway to cover up or find time just because I need extra time. But my tennis coach understands, so sometimes he would not let me play and I read and do my things instead. I can talk with him about my classmates and things that happened in my class. It is fun. I get a mental break. I knew that I would not become a tennis player, but I am a reasonably decent player winning something occasionally, so why shouldn't I have a good time?

My tennis coach is not mocking me every day, but he would call me "a baby elephant" occasionally. If I am too slow in doing my rounds he sometimes throws a tennis ball at me to speed me up. My sister would also laugh, so the thing is kind of funny for them, when he tries to make me run faster. But I just can't pull any competitiveness from me. I don't get it. I like tennis, but I just like to play and hit the ball – I don't like to participate in any race or run faster. It is just not my thing.

When I am in school, I am at rest. I score marks easily, so I am not under stress while I am in school. My teachers like me and even though I don't have a very strong social circle in school, partly because my parents don't allow me to interact with school friends beyond school hours. Sleepovers are not allowed, because they take us away from the schedule basically. So, I don't have a social circle, but I am with a few friends and they like me in general, so I feel good. I am involved in a lot of things. I contribute and volunteer for exhibitions. I participate in debates and quizzing teams. It's my life. It is everything. I sing in a prayer choir. I eventually became the perfect leader and held the school captain position. I enjoy everything with school. I like everything! I take it very positively and I am in more than everything I can possibly be in. I love those hours.

My LBL with Ketki

*Over the last years, I have had this feeling of being
constantly exhausted. I get plenty of time to rest
and have been sleeping more than I ever did
in any other place. It seemed like the exhaustion
was coming from some other place.
I could never get enough rest to recover.
Reading this transcription of my LBL has given me
a sudden realization. It's almost like
my soul was exhausted.*

KETKI

Ketki was 33 years old when she came for an LBL spiritual regression with me in the autumn of 2018. She is an engineer and researcher who was born in India. Ketki lives with her husband and daughter.

I was very impressed by Ketki from the start, because she seemed to be very mature, brilliant with words and wise. To facilitate her LBL was a true honor and a wonderful experience. I was so happy when she agreed to cooperate with me in this book project. It has been a pleasure to continue to communicate with her after the session, as well. She has taken her time and made the effort to send me many follow up texts.

Her reason for coming was to better understand her current life situation and relation to her family history. Her question was: "What is the main reason for this chosen life?" She also told me that she was very unhappy, because of her parent's divorce a few years ago. Her father had recently been diagnosed with terminal cancer. Since early childhood she wanted to please both her parents and cope with her sister who was hard for her to deal with. Her question was how she could help herself in all this, because she wanted to find contentment.

During the deepening stages of childhood memories in her LBL, Ketki spoke as the twelve-year-old ambitious young girl who loved going to school and handling her circumstances. Dr. Newton recommended going to childhood and to reconnect with happy memories as a "warming up" technique before going to even deeper memories in the womb before birth, where most often the clients seem to speak from a deeper level of the soul. This technique helps the client build positive resources and it makes the body and mind relax even more. The following dialogue is with Ketki telling me what it's like inside the womb of her mother before her birth into her present life. At this stage, she is deeply hypnotized.

Rita: Can I ask you if you feel eager to soon be born?

Ketki: *Yes, I am eager.*

R: What is your general impression of your mother?

K: *She is nervous.*

R: In which month do you enter your new hosting body with your soul?

K: *Towards the end. In the seventh month.*

R: When you enter the new hosting body in this way with your soul, do you have a feeling that you stay all the time or do you go back and forth?

K: *My feeling is that I stay, because she needs me.*

R: What can you now sense about her? Does she feel familiar to you?

K: *She is very familiar. I feel that she is "creating me" for a very strong purpose.*

R: Oh, really? Tell me more!

K: *She is putting everything in me. Her ambition, her future, all her hopes and everything into that womb of hers. Her future depends on it. I mean, it depends on Ketki.*

R: I can see from your tears that you are emotionally moved. What is happening to you now?

K: *It is like she is in a dark place and she feels that the light is going to come through me.*

R: Do you feel that you are coming to her willingly?

K: *Yes! With a lot of love, concern and care.*

R: You tell me also that she feels familiar.

K: *It feels like I have come on her calling.*

R: So, you said yes to her calling? Or how do you mean?

K: *It seemed very natural. I said yes immediately.*

R: Here you are now in the womb and you are soon going to be born. Let me ask you a few questions about your new hosting body Ketki, if it is okay. Do you as a soul find your new body easy to cooperate with? Is it a good match for your soul?

K: *Yes!*

R: What do you think about the brain? Is it well functioning?

K: *Very emotional.*

R: Okay, what do you mean by that?

K: *It is sensitive to emotions.*

R: Is it highly sensitive or becomes easily emotional and in touch with feelings?

K: *Both. Yes, I can sense the changes in my mother very quickly. I can also react and express my feelings very well.*

R: How do you feel about your own development? Can you tell me what it was like in the womb during the pregnancy?

K: *Yes, it seems that I am taking care of her.*

R: Thank you for telling me all this. Is there something else concerning your own hosting body that you would like to tell me?

K: *No, it seems perfect!*

R: What about your female body?

K: *Seems that I have chosen a gender to empathize better with her troubles. Because I need to set some things right. The battle must be fought from the weaker side.*

R: What do you mean?

K: *It would not mean that much if it was from a male perspective, because listening to a male is a natural order of things. Not because he is right or wrong, but because of him having to be heard is the order of things where she is being born right now. I must be heard as a female and to be valued as a female. Eventually we will all be valued as people, not as male or female.*

R: Can you tell me something more about the people around your mother and how you will relate to them when you are born?

K: *I know those people, but they are not my group. They are more like her problem, her group, her things. I am just here for her. It is her stage.*

R: Oh, you are calling it her stage. What is your role with her then?

K: *Support. Because she has chosen a very difficult journey.*

R: So, you are coming as a daughter, but you will also be here as her support. Have I understood what you mean here?

K: *As her daughter, because I will live longer with her as a daughter. I must live long enough to support her throughout* *her life. Especially when things get tougher in old age. It would be better for me to be younger than her.*

R: So, you are already preparing for the future. And you tell me that you are here for your mother? You heard her calling and came gladly. Did I get it right?

K: *Yes.*

R: Please tell me if there is any more information we can have now during this time in the womb. Something more you would like to share?

K: *I feel she chose a more difficult life than what was required. She chose many challenges and that's why she needs my support.*

R: I understand. What else is there to know now?

K: *I am thinking of other ways to try to make this impactful, because I am going to have a journey of my own. I am beginning to see the role of the female in the kind of society that she has chosen to be born in. I think that choosing to be a female is giving another opportunity to do and prove things, so I am trying if I can choose some journey for myself along the way.*

R: Did you have a soul agreement before you were born?

K: *Seems like we are done now. I think Ketki's job with her is almost over. She will be the loving companion for the mother, but I think that she has done well.*

R: Yes, Ketki seems to have done well!

K: *Now she will be there for me!*

R: That sounds very nice.

Past life memories

During our lives, all of us will experience
opportunities for change which involve risk.
These occasions may come at inconvenient times.
We may not act upon them, but the challenge is
there for us. The purpose of reincarnation
is the exercise of free will. Without this ability,
we would be impotent creatures indeed.

Michael Newton,

Journey of Souls: Case Studies of Life Between Lives

As I wrote before, Ketki was giving me the impression of a brilliant woman with great wisdom and knowledge. When her past life personality "Pravin" is speaking in the following dialogue and with Ketki even deeper hypnotized, he (Pravin) seems to be quite a different kind of personality than Ketki. He is verbally slow and doesn't seem to be as bright and emotional as Ketki. He also handles things very differently. Often

Ketki being Pravin was just quiet when I asked a question and I had to draw every word out of him. He seemed to be a very slow thinker in contrast to Ketki.

Rita: Please tell me about your feet now?

Ketki: *I have brown shoes with shoelaces, rounded fronts and backs. They are a little dusty.*

R: Do you have a feeling about the size of your feet?

K: *There are socks and they look like a grown child's feet, not sure.*

R: Please tell me more about your clothing, if possible.

K: *Brown trousers. Brown shirt, like those of a boy soldier. Like a uniform.*

R: What kind of uniform?

K: *A soldier's uniform. It is khaki color.*

R: Tell me about your hair.

K: *I am wearing a hat.*

R: What kind of hat?

K: *A round hat.*

R: Can you explain what is going on now in more detail?

K: *Like the soldiers in India, that kind of hat.*

R: Can you tell me the color of your skin?

K: *Can't say.*

R: Are you in the army?

K: *No, it's a police thing.*

R: Are you a female or a male?

K: *I think it is a male.*

R: Please take me now to a situation when you are dressed like this and tell me what happens.

K: *It seems that I am stationed outside some wall. It is outside a prison wall.*

R: What's your job?

K: *I am a guard.*

R: How old are you?

K: *19*

R: So, you are a young man.

K: *Yes.*

R: How do you feel in your body?

K: *I am alert.*

R: Do you hold on to something?

K: *No. There is a long gun on my back. It has a sharp knife at the end. I just stand there and people are moving around me. It looks like they are marching. Does not seem like an important role to play. I just stand here.*

R: So, what is your job, except standing there? Do you know what your job is?

K: *I think I am a prison guard.*

R: Thank you. Do you like it?

K: *I am indifferent.*

R: Do you have feelings?

K: *No.*

R: How are your days?

K: *I only know that I am standing here right now. There is a black gate. I feel so warm now!*
Ketki takes off her blanket, seems to feel hot suddenly.

R: What kind of gate is it?

K: *It is the prison gate. It looks like those old castles in India. A high concrete wall and a circular black gate. I just stand in front of it. So, it seems I am in British India. I think I am working for the British. Seems like it.*

R: Okay.

K: *It seems like green fields all around.*

R: Can we now go forward a few years in your life and see what happens? How many years can we roll forward?

K: *I don't know.*

R: Do you feel a little indifferent about it? How does your brain function in this body?

K: *I am not much of a thinker.*

R: Aha. What more is there to know about the person you are now?

K: *Does not feel much either. Do not feel too much about anything.*

R: So, now you are in British India. Let's now go to the last day and moment of your life. But first, please tell me your name if possible.

K: *The first name that comes to my mind is Pravin.*

R: Can I now call you Pravin?

K: *Yes.*

Moment of death
and crossing over into the spirit world

*Oversoul Seven grimaced at Cyprus and began
the examination. 'Let's see,' he said, 'In Earth terms,
using an analogy, I'm a man on Wednesday and
Friday, a woman on Sunday and Thursday, and
have the rest of the time off for independent study.*

JANE ROBERTS:

THE OVERSOUL SEVEN TRILOGY

Newton was working with thousands of clients over many decades. He found that there was a consistency in what his clients experienced after the death moment in a past life. He created a method which simplified for his clients to have a kind of near death-experience(NDE) during induced hypnotic theta brain wave trance. His method is characterized by first going to a past life and then to the last day and moment of the past life and then leaving the dead body behind and crossing over to the spirit world. It seemed to him that most of his clients quite easily, if they were in deep trance, could enter the spirit world from the "front door" as he called entering the afterlife from the death moment in a past life. If we have died many times, the soul remembers the experience, he gathered.

After my training and my first own LBL, I personally found his theory to work in practice. Since 2013 most of my clients describe their own death moment in a past life. Over the years, I have met clients who had a very strong fear of death, but after the LBL the fear faded away to some extent, some of them told me. The past life character Pravin dies from getting crushed in a stampede by the age of 21. During this part of the session I ask Ketki, deeply hypnotized, how it feels. Pravin is not very talkative, but just gives me short and polite answers. It seems his personality is the same after he died.

Rita: Pravin, can you please go to the last day of your life? Where are you now and what happens? Tell me first how old you are, if you know.

Ketki: *I am 21!*

R: What is going on?

K: *A stampede. People are rushing around, like a crowd running around. It is a riot and people are dying because they are being stepped on.*

R: Like a chaotic situation?

K: *Yes.*

R: What is happening to you?

K: *Getting crushed.*

R: Is your death coming unexpectedly or do you have time to feel fear?

K: *It seems this is the atmosphere of the time. These things keep happening. I kind of expected to insignificantly go away like this.*

R: So, Pravin you have just died, and this you have done many times. You will be able to continue talking with me as a soul now. How do you feel about your own death as Pravin?

K: *I am okay with it!*

R: Do you know your way as a soul now or do you want to check on something before your return to soul home?

K: *I think I know the way! Seems like the whole purpose was just to fill out some numbers there. I mean, we needed some people to go there and die, so I was not expected to achieve much. It is like "head counts".*

R: What was the purpose of this short life from the perspective of your soul?

K: *A lot of us had to do it, because when there is a war for independence and these sorts of things, a lot of young people die. To change things for the future, you must be born and die quickly many times. There is nothing to achieve except the transition that comes afterwards. At least for me, there was nothing to do. There were no bonds.*

R: So, now as a soul you are free to return to your soul home? Do you feel that you know the way? Or somebody comes to meet you?

K: *I think I know the way.*

R: How exciting. Please let me know how you travel.

Orientation after crossing over

After the death moment and crossing over into the afterlife the soul is open for a moment of reflection and orientation. Most often this happens together with the primary guide of the client who comes to meet the returning soul. In the following dialogue, I try to figure out what happens with the soul after Pravin dies. In this case, there is no guide coming to meet the returning soul. I am informed by the soul that it knows the way by itself. Instead, in the case with Ketki the soul of her present husband turns up in this moment after crossing over. She explains her version of this in a letter to me a year after the session.

"During the session, I felt like some parts of this soul experience were intentionally blocked by a higher energy. I wanted to meet my guides and looked for them, but they chose to stay away. This has also been the case in the one year following this LBL. Whenever I seek my guide, I get a message saying, "not yet". I have now accepted that I must grow more in this life, to seek

them. I draw an analogy with my four-year-old daughter. Sometimes she asks me questions which are valid and genuine, but I must tell her that I cannot answer before she is older. Because she is not there yet. I assure her of the validity of her question and provide some thoughts about it, but I do not give answers. I feel I am like a four-year-old in the spiritual world. My guide, just like a parent, is kindly withholding some parts, because it is not yet the right time. However, they have always provided me with assurance and positive thoughts, through Rita, or my husband or other friendly companions."

Michael Newton had a theory that we, as souls, are both in soul home and in the present or perhaps even in several incarnations at the same time. In his books, he calls it "soul energy" and based on this theory he asked all his LBL clients the question: "Which percentage of your total soul energy did you bring into this present (and past life) incarnation?" The most common answer I have heard from my clients is 15–80%. Why is this question relevant, you might ask? When we die, we seem to go back to the soul home and reunite with the remaining part of the soul energy. This way we become whole again in our nonphysical soul identity in life between lives. In my book *To soul home and back* I write more about this, but I recommend you read the books by Dr. Newton if you are interested to learn his theories from the source.

Rita: What was the purpose of your life as Pravin?

Ketki: *A lot of us had to descend to earth, because when there is war for independence and that sort of thing, a lot of young people die. To change things for the future you must many times be born and die quickly. There is nothing to achieve except the transition that comes afterwards. At least for me there was nothing to do. There were no bonds.*

R: Now as a soul you are free to return to your soul home. Do you feel that you know the way? Or does anybody meet you?

K: *I think I know the way.*

R: So, now you will still be able to continue to speak with me and tell me what happens, even though you are now a nonphysical being after you died as Pravin.

K: *I feel very happy now!*

R: Where are you going now?

K: *I go through bright yellowish white light. I am swimming towards it and I am cool about it.*

R: Please try to explain what happens!

K: *Does not seem like I needed a cleansing after returning. It was a very short life. I don't see any cleansing. I just joined* *the white light. Feels like I have gone to sleep, because it seems like an exhausting day of work. You go through your routine day and you finish off and at night you are tired. This I can feel from my soul's perspective. It was like a day's work. Not a lifetime's work. It was not troublesome. It did not hurt too much. Just had to go in there and get it done. So, now I am kind of resting from the effort.*

R: I see! Thank you.

We identify as one

The user can share pieces of their soul with other persons. By filling part of the recipient's soul with their own piece of soul the user can even heal the recipient's physical, mental and spiritual wounds that wouldn't normally heal on their own.

UNKNOWN AUTHOR

After crossing over from the death moment and changing into a nonphysical state, perhaps a cleansing takes place. Then the journey into the afterlife continues with a reflection from the soul about the life they just left on earth. It is always very exciting to hear my client describe in detail what they experience along the way. Ketki tells me a lot at this stage. She is not met by a primary guide like many of my clients, but by the soul of her husband who she says is another part of her soul. Could it be that they are one and the same soul, like she says?

Rita: Please let me know what you experience now.

Ketki: *I see some other energies. I don't see. I feel it. They are more like equal energies. I am back with my friends. But I don't really recognize anything. It is a feeling that everything is being pulled towards me and we just relax together.*

R: Just enjoy it now if you want!

K: *I feel I am some sort of intermediate soul.*

R: What do you mean by that?

K: *I have done well in the basic levels, but I must start taking up more responsibility related things among my peers to start off with. I think I got a hang of the routine things.*

R: What are the routine things?

K: *Being born and doing well generally on regular virtues, like doing well for myself alone. But now I must move to something more than myself. It is doing well for oneself despite having responsibility. I got to learn those things and it is going to start, not with mentoring other people or like mentoring juniors or something. I am going to be helping friends.*

R: Do you have a feeling to have something in common as souls with these other energies you are with now?

K: *We are all intermediate. But we have shown good progress. We are ready for some bigger lessons.*

R: How do you feel about that then?

K: *Enthusiastic! Challenged, but I am up for it.*

R: Do you feel like staying or moving on now?

K: *I go to a green place. It is like a little garden.*

R: Do you go alone or do you have someone with you?

K: *There seems to be someone who goes with me.*

R: Do you know if this someone is a female or male or maybe genderless?

K: *I think they are all genderless, but I have a feeling it is my husband in my present life.*

R: Oh, okay. What about him?

K: *We are friends. He feels like a friend.*

R: Do you know if this soul who is your husband in your present life also incarnated in the life of Pravin?

K: *I don't think so. He was not there. It was not needed.*

R: So, now you are in a garden with the soul you recognize as the soul of your husband in your present life as Ketki. Tell me some more, please!

K: *It seems that he and I are two manifestations of the same thing.*

R: What do you mean?

K: *I feel that we combine energies and we do things together.*

R: Interesting!

K: *We don't necessarily split, but we split into two this time.*

R: Can you help me understand what kind of soul relationship you have?

K: *We identify as one.*

R: Can you tell me now what happens in the garden?

K: *The place is greenish, because we are all greenish.*

R: What does this mean?

K: *We find it pleasant to look at things like that.*

R: What kind of green is it?

K: *It is the shade of grass in spring.*

R: Does this color have a deeper impact for Ketki as a soul as well?

K: *I think it reflects our growth level.*

R: Do you know if you have a soul characteristic based on this color and the frequencies in the color?

K: *Yes, I think we have reached calmness. But it seems that the calm component is in his half. So, if we separate out the twin soul thing, then he is the calm component. If we are together, we are the right mix of emotion and calm. Very balanced!*

R: So, what is your component?

K: *Sensitivity to feelings.*

R: Okay, so together you cooperate in a certain way. Does it happen that you incarnate without each other?

K: *Yes. I don't know why I said that, but we do.*

R: In your life as Ketki you both incarnated and met. But not in the Pravin life?

K: *Seems like I was learning not to feel in the Pravin life.*

R: I see. You also have told me that the life of Pravin was an incarnation when it was about just counting the heads. Tell me more, please.

K: *It's like you need ten people to die in this transition, so you just raise like ten chickens in a farm. You know that they are going to be killed like that.*

R: Can you tell me a little bit more about this?

K: *There are battles and people die and that battle is necessary, because life happens on the other side. A lot of people are born and you don't really plan for them to grow older and have things happening as life lessons in their 50's or 60's. If they are raised to be slaughtered, you just count 100 of them or 200 of them. It is a "head count".*

R: Oh, really? Do you know if they incarnate voluntarily based on free will? Please tell me more about this!

K: *Yes, they do. Because someone must go through the transition and usually the ones who are not afraid of dying volunteer. We don't keep too many attachments unless someone has something to learn and we could use their experience. Mostly it is like for Pravin who did not have anybody and he did not leave anybody behind. There was no fear of death. He knew how to separate those things out. It did not matter. So, I, as a soul, had to get rid of the feelings for a while.*

R: What could be the reason for the British rule in India and all the people dying like Pravin in the situation?

K: *The war was needed to relieve India, and that would not have happened without the deaths of many people. Transition is painful! Sometimes things need to change. This is needed in a person's life, but also on a national level.*

R: How interesting. Thank you for telling me all this!

Parents and the divorce

Ketki told me about her feelings of guilt and shame from early childhood. These feelings were making her exhausted, because she was under a lot of pressure as a child and young adult. Now she wanted to find a way to break free from her father who had pressured her since she was a little child. Becoming a young adult, she supported her mother in the decision to finally divorce. When additionally, her father was diagnosed with terminal cancer, Ketki did not know how to deal with the situation which had become so filled with guilt for her. She felt it was time to take a stand. She came to her LBL filled with doubts. She told me that she wanted to find out how to handle her difficult life situation the best possible way. With Ketki deeply hypnotized we could ask the questions so important for her.

Rita: I'd like to ask you now about the divorce of the parents of Ketki, because at one point you said that it is not the father who is the point, it is the mother. Is there anything else now that you realize as a soul which could free Ketki from her concerns and responsibility concerning her parents?

Ketki: *Feeling concern is a natural quality of my soul, so it really has nothing to do with the father or anybody. It is her spirit's inherent quality to feel that way, and I should look at it as my strength, not as a weakness or something that is holding me back. However, feeling concern and feeling responsibility are different things.*

Life purpose and mission

My clients often tell me that they would like to know their life purpose and mission. It seems to me that some of them believe it is a struggle, but it seems to be the greatest joy to fulfill a life purpose by doing what we love. Ketki told me she wanted relief from her feelings of guilt and shame.

It seems the purpose of life becomes clearer when we let go of guilt, shame and fear. Then there is a path suddenly opening, just waiting for us to see it. The life purpose most often is revealed in stages and with timing. In LBL-sessions the soul often talks about its present ongoing incarnation and character in third person, like Ketki does in the dialogues. From her soul's perspective Ketki is just another incarnation, like Pravin.

Rita: Can you tell me something about what all this means for Ketki?

Ketki: *It's all about awareness! We are in a new stage of evolution. That's good. We are learning about our common power as a group and as a collective consciousness. We are* *learning how to reverse negative changes with collective consciousness. I think it's a strength. A few years back we did not know that we had that energy and our collective conscience led to negative changes or damages to the earth. But now as a population we are learning to use it in a positive sense. We are harnessing the energy. We will learn to ride it soon.*

R: Is there anything more we need to investigate now about your present life?

K: *I have reached a point in life where I must detach from certain things to pursue certain other things. I have completed many tasks and I must not hold on to the scars. They were good, they were bad, but they were both necessary. The new chapter is for a different purpose. This was a transition and every transition is painful. Like the one with Pravin coming and then dying in the transition.*

R: Can we get a little glimpse of the future for Ketki?

K: *She will stay away from the limelight. It will be at grassroots level.*

R: What is the reason for this?

K: *The contentment. It is not about fame or power. It is like growing tomatoes in your own garden.*

R: Because if you as Ketki would be a leader who would have to confront …

K: *… it will take her away from the purpose.*

R: Please tell me more about this.

K: *I think I know now. My father presented me like a trophy daughter and he pushed me to be the number one. I got my fame as a child with my name in the newspaper and it showed me what I did not want.*

R: That's an amazing realization.

K: *I have seen that side where I am recognized in my school as a champion. When I had my photo in the press and in the hallways and people celebrating me, I realized that I don't want it. I don't work for it anymore. If I had not had it, I would crave it thinking that that's the end goal and that there is happiness in it for me. But now I know early on that it's not there. I have already been there.*

R: What is all this about for you?

K: *Instinct. Learning. Guidance.*

R: Can you feel now what is happening?

K: *I am feeling good! I think I am like a perfectly baked chocolate pastry!*

A higher power and a guiding force

She just needs to know that there is a higher power.
That there is a guiding force. She needs to know
that there are times when things become
overwhelming and most importantly that
there is a bigger picture. It is not necessarily
the impact of previous deaths or the journey
or the partner, but just the fact
that such a journey exists.

KETKI

Ketki was a very ambitious young girl. When she came to see me by the age of 33 she gave herself permission to relax and start living a happier life with self-love and acceptance following the guidance from her soul. Her LBL facilitated a life with contentment rather than guilt, shame and fear which was preventing her from enjoying her life. When she connected with her deeper self and soul, she felt a higher power and guiding force from within. Her own truth became clear to her, considering that only a few hours in a deep hypnotic state can be so life changing. When the timing for the soul is right, many things fall in place.

A letter from Ketki
a few months after her session

The concept of family

As a child, one's whole world revolves around the few people they live with.

We do not see the universe beyond those people (parents, siblings). Their approval, acceptance and love seem to be the basis of one's existence.

Happiness depends a lot on what we receive from them (praise, trust, love, security). Now I realize that all human beings are one family. My true family, my soul group, my companions, are everywhere, not biologically related to me (to my current physical form). My happiness does not and should not depend on the acceptance of a few people. I carry the source of happiness within me. My love is not restricted to parents or siblings. Love cannot be restricted like that. It is free flowing, to give and receive. You cannot force anyone to love you and you cannot love anyone out of compulsion. There is no guilt in loving someone more than those related to you by blood.

To give you an analogy of this feeling: "I had planted a flower in my window. All these years I watered, nurtured and gave it all my love and energy, hoping that the flowers of happiness will one day blossom. I waited for years, never losing faith and never relaxing my efforts, pouring my soul into it. Occasionally, a small bud would show up and it would rejuvenate me, thinking that the flower of happiness is about to bloom! However, the bud would wither away, without blooming. Often, there were only thorns and no flowers. Over the years, my soul got exhausted from the effort. You cannot pour from an empty cup. I needed to refill my energy.

After all, the flower is going to bloom any day now! That's when this LBL-session happened. I was so engrossed in the plant, that I forgot to look outside. There I saw an entire garden, growing in the wild, filled with all kinds of flowers, not just happiness, but love, joy, grace, beauty and acceptance. That garden had been there all along. Those flowers were mine to cherish and they didn't ask anything in return."

All this, while I gave my everything to my family and chased their love, to find my happiness. I looked within the four walls of my home and thought that the entire universe exists within it. Now I realize that there are no boundaries. There is a lot of love waiting for me outside. My family is not just four people. It is every soul that I feel connected with.

I feel liberated.

~

PART 4

The importance of purposeful friends

~

*Now I feel a freedom,
hope and joy to complete the mission.
But it will need others!*

TERRY EVANS

I can never trust her

I am six or seven years old now. I don't blame her, but I cannot trust her. She never keeps her promises. She doesn't know how to. I am not angry with her. I feel sad for her.

I try to take care of her. Why does she let him beat me? Why does she not believe me? Why, why, why? She never listens. I don't hate her. I just don't trust her.

He is struggling. He is angry. He is confused.

Oh, he is smiling. The final thing. Release. He is so curious. So many questions. He is blond. He is secretive. He does not tell everybody everything. He does not tell anyone about the shadows. Or the things he sees. It stays with him.

My LBL with Terry Evans

It took me five years to finish my first book *To soul home and back*. At times when I had given up hope on the project, suddenly somebody magically showed up and helped me carry on and complete my book. My first encounter with Terry Evans was quite mind-blowing. We had never met, but still the first thing he said when he saw me was: "When are you going to finish your book?" Although I knew about Terry being a famous clairvoyant here in Sweden, I was surprised he seemed to sense that I was stuck in my writing.

I had heard about him from several of my LBL-clients over the years. They told me about his excellent spiritual medium courses and readings. Many had also met him when he performed his clairvoyant and healing skills for hundreds of people in psychic evenings and clairvoyant demonstrations all around Sweden. I had also seen him on a Swedish TV show called "The unknown", where psychics show their abilities to declutter haunted houses. Terry's interest in parapsychology and mediumship began at an early age. His first encounter with an actual spiritualist medium came at the age of 22, when he was given his first private consultation by a medium. The effects of that experience became a turning point in his life, offering new realizations. These realizations motivated him to develop his own inner potential of mediumship and intuition.

I was later invited by Terry to give lectures and workshops about LBL at his center and was very happy for his help and support in my work. Terry is a hardworking and very kind man. In so many ways he teaches others about the soul and the spirit world and helps people understand the human experience from a higher perspective. So, naturally I was happy to facilitate his LBL in 2018. He already had a strong connection and clear communication with his spirit guide Ascala since he was young, so I wondered what he could possibly gain from an LBL.

However, he told me that he had a very rewarding session. Terry has kindly given me his permission to use his session and real name. This is unusual, because my oath of silence in my profession does not allow me to reveal any of my client's real names. Terry has himself shared his LBL-experience with his followers on social media and other platforms, so in this way he also helped promote my work in so many ways.

Dear Terry, I thank you deeply for your support and loving kindness!

A past life in Germany

Terry easily regressed to his early childhood years when he told me how he felt about his mother as a six-year-old boy. He simultaneously seemed to understand his mother from his soul perspective as presented with the monologue in the beginning of this chapter.

The regression to childhood is like a warming up to help the client go deeper into relaxation step by step and then eventually reach the death moment in a past life. In my past life as Leyla I died when I suffocated with a peach seed stuck in my throat. Pravin died from being crushed in a stampede. These are all examples of ways clients experience their death moment. In this dialogue, Terry tells me about a past life in Germany and how he died.

Rita: So, you are travelling in time now?

Terry: *Yes. I am in Berlin.*

R: Please tell me what you perceive now.

T: *I was hit by a bus or a tram. I am lying down.*

R: Who are you now?

T: *GERHART! GERHART!*

R: What happened?

T: *Nein, nein, das ist nicht gut, nein, nein, nein. I need to get up. I cannot lie in the street.*

R: Is Gerhart your name?

T: *Yes.*

R: Tell me what happened!

T: *I was daydreaming, I wasn't there. I was not paying attention. I was in my mind. I always was in my mind. My papers are everywhere. I dropped my papers.*

R: Where are you now when you were hit by the bus?

T: *I am at Feltham Strasse.*

R: I see! How do you feel now?

T: *I'm numb.*

R: In your whole body?

T: *Yes, my papers are everywhere.*

R: So, tell me what happens now?

Terry makes a sound like a long "swish" and his back is lifting from the couch for a short while and he looks very tense and agitated.

R: What happened? Did you leave your body, Gerhard?

T: *Hm ...*

R: What happens now?

T: *I am fighting.*

R: As a soul, tell me what happens now.

T: *I am looking down.*

R: What do you see?

T: *It is difficult to take my body from underneath the bus, or is it a tram? It's a tram! It is a horse drawn tram.*

R: How do you feel about your own death?

T: *Sad.*

R: Can you tell me why?

T: *Did not finish my work.*

R: How old are you when you die?

T: *I am 22.*

Crossing over after death in the accident

Even though I have witnessed it many times in my work as an LBL-facilitator, it is always quite a surreal sensation to hear through the voice of my clients when they tell me how it is to die in a past life. Terry has a natural talent to explain this clearly, because as a medium he is used to going into a deep altered state of relaxation quite easily and to talk from there. Now he starts telling me what happens after he is run over by the tram and dies.

Rita: What happened now?

Terry: *Just floating.*

R: Please let me know what happens, so I can accompany you where you are going. Do you know your way now?

T: *I know my way. I have been here before.*

R: Do you feel eager to go?

T: *No, I am sad that I did not finish my work.*

R: I am sorry.

T: *I MUST finish my work! I MUST finish my work!*

R: Is it possible to share what this work that you must finish is all about?

T: *It is solving problems.*

R: What kind of problems? In what field?

T: *It's science. To help people. It's about how the mind works.*

R: Is this the work you need to finish?

T: *Ja, ja, ja, ja.*

R: Please tell me a bit more about this work. If you feel like it, you can share with me.

T: *I am only interested in working, but nobody will listen to what I say.*

R: Can you tell me what the date is now when you die, Gerhart?

T: *1902, April 12.*

R: Thank you. What happens to you now?

T: *I want to stay. But they are calling me.*

R: Why do you want to stay?

T: *I have gone to a cloud now.*

Going home after a life

This is a dialogue with Terry in a deep altered state of consciousness. He is speaking about "a place of higher learning" and tells me about going through a tunnel after the moment of death. Many people who had a near death-experience also describe their death the same way.

Terry: *Now it is quicker and quicker. Faster and faster. I have been here. I know this tunnel. I am not afraid of this tunnel. Suddenly I slowed down.*

Rita: Yes. Very good. Please tell me what you perceive now.

T: *I am in a place of learning.*

R: Is it possible to describe it for me, please?

T: *It's not about another lifetime!*

R: Okay!

T: *I know this place.*

R: Please tell me what you experience.

T: *I am just waiting. I cannot allow myself to be pushed.*

R: I will wait!

T: *We had to bring you back.*

R: Who are the "we" telling you this?

T: *The masters, the teachers.*

Another incarnation during war times

Sometimes the client experiences more than one past life in one session. Terry returns to a life in Germany after his visit to the place of higher learning. Here is a dialogue starting with his soul still in the learning place. He talks about what happens before it is time for his soul to incarnate again for another life on earth.

Terry: *Just resting! I am not going to be staying here long. I am back in Germany again. I am Robert Schmitt now.*

Rita: Robert Schmitt?

T: *Ja, ja.*

R: What year is it now?

T: *1937.*

R: Okay, so tell me what is going on? Where are you now?

T: *I hear shouting and screaming.*

R: Are you alone or in a crowd?

T: *It is terror. I can see the swastika. It's the "Third Reich?"*

R: So, people are screaming. Are you screaming as well?

T: *I am not screaming. I am observing. Just watching.*

R: I see, okay. Can you feel what age you are now?

T: *I am 14 years old.*

R: So, you are a young boy?

T: *I am nearly 15.*

R: I am curious to know what is going on here. Can you take me to a moment when something happens which is important for your soul to remember now?

T: *I cannot have this! I don't like to be told what to think! I am fighting.*

R: What do you mean by fighting?

T: *I mean physically.*

R: Do you have a strong and athletic body?

T: *I am okay, just keep fighting.*

R: With whom are you fighting?

T: *My father. I will not be in the Hitler-Jugend!*

R: So, he wants you to join them?

T: *No, nein, nein. I must go.*

R: Do they force you to go?

T: *Ja.*

R: What do they want you to do?

T: *I did not trust that man.*

R: Who?

T: *Adolf Hitler. I have the same feeling as before. I see things. I know things. They don't understand how I see and how I know.*

R: Can we go to the next significant moment in your life now as Robert Schmitt?

T: *It's war, I am a soldier. Wehrmacht. I keep quiet. I do what I must do.*

R: How old are you now?

T: *18 or 19.*

R: What is it like for you now?

T: *I do what I do.*

R: Do you have a girlfriend?

T: *No.*

R: What are you like, as a person?

T: *I do what I do, but I don't fit in.*

R: In what way?

T: *Now I must fight, but I don't want to do it.*

R: How are you dressed?

T: *In green uniform. I am a soldier.*

R: How do you cope with all this as a person?

T: *I just know how to. I am here. They have made me a leader.*

R: What kind of leader?

T: *I am a corporal now.*

R: Well, how does this feel now?

T: *I have no choice.*

R: What is your job?

T: *I am in the infantry.*

R: What happens?

T: *It was an explosion. Maybe a fire?*

R: How does the explosion or fire affect you?

T: *It damages my lungs.*

R: I am sorry to hear this. How is it going now?

T: *Not good.*

R: Can you still breathe? Not very well it seems from listening to your breath now.

Terry sounds like he is short of breath.

R: Where are you now?

T: *I am in a hospital.*

R: Can you tell me what happens? Were you taken to the hospital by someone?

T: *I don't remember. I woke up in the hospital. But I can remember the explosion. Thomas, my friend has passed.*

R: I am sorry. How are you now?

T: *I know I am going to pass.*

R: Why? Is your body damaged?

T: *Yes.*

R: How old are you now?

T: *I am 19.*

R: Is there anybody around you now?

T: *I don't have time.*

R: Have you already passed?

T: *I am leaving. I am back in the tunnel.*

R: Okay!

T: *It's a relief.*

Saying goodbye to Mutti

Most often the soul leaving a past life body on earth takes the opportunity to say goodbye to loved ones before the final departure to afterlife. Terry tells me how he, as a departed soul, reaches out to his mother and he calls her "Mutti", the German word for mother.

Rita: Anybody you left behind that you would like to say goodbye to now?

Terry: *Mutti.*

R: Oh, your mother?

T: *Mutti, dear. I can see that the clock on the wall is half past four.*

R: Do you know the soul of your Mutti?

T: *No.*

R: What was the meaning of this short life as Robert?

T: *To understand the brutality of war. Preparing me for the future. To give me understanding and insight. My lungs!*

R: What is it with your lungs?

T: *Ahhhh, I don't know.*

R: Do you feel like resting now?

T: *Okay.*

R: Is it possible to take a deep breath now, just to clear the lungs?

T: Exhales loudly.

R: Are you okay with leaving Mutti now?

T: *She is Frida. Her name is Frida.*

R: Can she sense you now when you come to say goodbye?

T: *No.*

R: What are the circumstances for her?

T: *She is sad, but she has a job to do.*

R: Okay, what is her job?

T: *She is like my father. They believe in Adolf Hitler.*

R: Oh, so she believes in him as well.

T: *She does not hear me. They are ruled by a tyrant. That is why I'd like to come home now.*

R: So, let's see what you need to do now as a soul.

T: *I am back again!*

R: Where are you now?

T: *I am back in the learning place.*

The place of higher learning

After the experience as a soldier, the soul of Terry seems to be very relieved to be back in what he calls the learning place. He meets his spirit guide Ascala. Here is how the dialogue unfolds:

Terry: *I am back now in the place of higher learning.*

Rita: That's nice. Do you sense any features of your soul?

T: *Everything about me is green. It is a beautiful green color.*

R: Wonderful. Is it a dark or a light green?

T: *It is an emerald green.*

R: Do you get a sense of what this color means for you as a soul?

T: *He tells me now! It's my heart. He takes me back. He reminds me of a life in China! My guide Ascala is talking now!*

R: How nice! What about China?

T: *I am happy. I am in a temple. He is preparing me. He is not going to keep me here long. He says: "You will not be here long."*

R: Is it possible to ask if there is anything we can know about the theme for your soul through incarnations and who you are as a soul?

T: *I am being prepared for the future.*

R: Do you mean in your present life as Terry?

T: *Yes, in Terry's life. Now I understand the diagrams and the things Terry was shown before.*

R: Would you like to share what you now understand?

T: *Terry remembers seeing a film many years ago: "Close encounters of a third kind." The main character gets this image of a mountain. Everybody thought he was crazy and nobody listened to him, but he found his mountain. He climbed to the top of this mountain. A spaceship communicated in colors. This green again. I was spellbound when I watched the film. Every second I was completely focused. Some years later Ascala started to talk with me about mountain meditation.*

R: Yes.

T: *And then I understood. This is a mountain that helps people. But there will be more. The signs. Ascala took me back to ancient China. I understand now. And I must work on how to connect to it.*

R: What is the purpose of remembering these two lives in Germany?

T: *To make me stronger. To survive that war. I went to a quiet place myself. I was there, but I was not there.*

R: We have met the little boy Terry who also often was in terror as a child. Is there anything this boy has in common with the young man in Germany not wanting to believe in Hitler.

T: *Neither one of us belonged. We had to learn to stand in between two worlds. The place I go to meet spirit, to go from my logical brain into that place of silence, is similar.*

R: I see. Thank you for explaining this to me.

T: *I had to understand about violence. All of us were on the side of society. That's where we had to be. We had to learn.*

R: What happens now?

T: *Now I understand. That was part of my mission. These were lifetimes of preparations for now. To learn how to endure* *and still stand my ground. To learn to say no and to face criticism. This I have had from sceptics in my lifetime as Terry. Especially from my stepfather. I must thank them too, because they were my teachers. It taught me about hatred and bitterness, and not to make the same mistake myself. To forgive. That's what I do now, I teach people to forgive themselves. To help them fulfill their mission. To keep their promise. It's hard work.*

R: It's hard work. Truly hard work. Thank you.

T: *When I leave this life, I won't be back. I will work from the other side. For quite a long time. I must get this mission completed. It must become a school. A place where people can go and find themselves.*

My Guide Ascala

Terry writes about Ascala:

Ascala is my guide, a part of the higher intelligence that lives within me. His job is to help me build a bridge to higher intelligence, the world which he comes from. When I work with him I cannot make demands. I just allow him to give me mind openers, to remind me who I am as a person. His job is also to help me fulfill my mission in the current incarnation. He carefully monitors my progression and when he feels I am ready to walk through another portal to higher intelligence, he will send me a challenge into my reality. My biggest challenge is to prevent my ego from taking over. He reminds me of what mediums said to me in my early days and what I would become if I followed his guidance. He spoke of many things I would do in the future. At the time, it was very hard to believe or accept. He is my friend, the voice of my soul, the voice of the higher intelligence that lives within every human being. He is also like my guardian angel and has many times intervened and literally saved my life. Without that guidance or intervention, I would not be here today. He is a living part of me and I am a living part of him. With each step we take, the most important challenge of all is that we continue to grow and come closer together, so that we can achieve the purpose of the incarnation in which I now live.

Terry is used to working with his guide Ascala since he was young. For many of my clients this is not the case. They tell me that they never connected with a spiritual guide. It is often overwhelming and a happy event to meet the primary soul guide in an LBL. When I met Alfred, I was very thankful and moved to tears. I could feel his loving presence so clearly and in my inner eye I saw him as well. This was a life changing experience on a very day-to-day practical level, because I could clearly sense he is my wise mediator between the worlds. Alfred is not the kind of guide who intervenes in my decisions, but when I turn to him and ask for advice he becomes very real to me. Feeling his presence calms me down and makes me peaceful and grounded.

Terry: *I have Ascala. He has always been with me. Always. He has been a part of my soul from the day my soul was created.*

Rita: That is fascinating. Please tell me more!

T: *I don't know how, but one day there's a flash of light. And my soul was created. Now I understand the quality. It was me so long ago, as a soldier. A roman soldier. Now I understand the cruelty of what people do. When they fight for their country, ha! That's why I had to go back to Germany.*

R: I really wonder what the meaning of suffering is. And if it is the only way of learning, as some say. Can you say something about suffering?

T: *Suffering is important for the soul. If we did not experience suffering, how can we understand? If we do not experience suffering, how can we help others? The soul's mission is to find identity and individual purpose and what they can offer. Nobody has the right to tell us what to believe and how to behave.*

R: Okay, so maybe when people remember or their souls remember, they are hopefully not so easily corrupted. Sometimes we are just forced to do something, like you had to become a soldier in the circumstance at the time. You were forced to do it, one could say.

T: *When I was a roman soldier, I enjoyed it.*

R: So, are you telling me now about yet another incarnation when you seemed to enjoy making people suffer?

T: *It feels like I am a warrior. A soldier. But I never get recognition. I enjoyed it.*

R: What did you enjoy the most as a roman soldier?

T: *It's the recognition which it is important for me to experience.*

R: Do you kill people?

T: *Yes, I kill people. I show no mercy. I don't want to kill anyone. Now I understand.*

R: What do you understand?

T: *My childhood with my stepfather. He did terrible things. I feel sad to suffer like that. He would not have understood. So, what comes around, goes around.*

R: I'd like to know if there are others at the place of higher learning which you told me about? Do you have a soul group or a group of others that you connect with, or are you alone?

T: *You are there.*

R: What?

T: *You are there.*

R: Aha, so I am there. So, what do we do there?

— 155 —

T: *Sometimes we get into trouble. Not in a bad way.*

R: Really?

R: What do we have in common with the souls who are there?

T: *We have been trained to serve humanity. We have chosen to do this work.*

Opportunities to heal with LBL

Most LBL-sessions are very healing and often a huge feeling of general relief occurs during and after the experience. With 3–4 hours of deep relaxation in an altered state of hypnosis the person becomes very receptive to changing their world-view after understanding themselves from a higher perspective. This most often brings healing to the client and it is an introduction to meet and get to know their own soul identity. When the conscious mind steps aside, the brain can work its magic by sending out a lot of healing substances like oxytocin and noradrenalin into the body. This happened to me in my LBL with Dorothea. It also happens to Terry by the end of his session.

Rita: I'd like to know if there is anything that can be healed in the physical body of Terry, while you as a soul have all these insights.

Terry: *There's sadness. I am sad sometimes. Just sad by the way people behave. So disappointed. That is my biggest* *sadness. I still have that problem from the journey as a soldier in Germany and from Gerhart. I still have that problem. Why do people behave like this?*

R: Please tell me more about your sadness.

T: *It is almost like a sadness of the soul.*

R: Yes, this sounds convincing to me. I understand.

T: *It's like a curse, the sadness. I am learning to live with it. But I'd like to be stronger. I'd like to … but I am sad … by the way people treat one another. How they behave. It saddens my soul. But I have decided to see it as the way humanity is. I can't change humanity. But maybe I can have an effect simply by what I do?*

R: If you allow my reflection here. Maybe it can be one of the facets of your psychic abilities to see through people in a way they cannot see themselves. You see their hidden treasure of gold and their darkness, but the person will sometimes never come to realize or see their own hidden treasures and shadows.

T: *Some do, some don't. It's like Jesus said: "You cannot cast pearls before swine."*

R: And he also said that you must come as a child to enter heaven.

T: *I haven't forgotten how to play.*

R: What happened to the joy?

T: *Today I found it again!*

R: I am happy to hear this.

T: *It's coming back. People are coming into my life now. Like you, Rita. Sounds crazy, but to go back to these three lifetimes, I am not angry with my mother anymore. I accept her. I understand that she did not have a choice either. It's how she was. One thing I can share with you. When they took her to spirit, first she was in denial. They worked on her. She had to accept, even though she tried to escape, she left with cancer. When she got to the other side, she had to realize what an effect she had on me and others. She tried to come near me and I said: "No, you must go, you can't stay here. You have to go on." And then they showed me the help I was now giving her. How she resisted, even there, she was in denial. But, she came through. Now she works with me. Today in a meditation I said: "Mama, now I can really let this go. I have peace with you now".*

R: Wonderful. I am happy for you!

T: *Now I feel a freedom, hope and joy to complete the mission. But it will need others.*

R: You have all these connections and they will gravitate towards you, I am sure.

T: *As you have. Because when you came I just knew, without you telling me, that you were drawn to me for some reason. I was thinking why was this lady drawn to me? But you are here. You were the only one that could take me on this journey.*

R: I am grateful for the opportunity.

T: *But I must say this. My real home, the place we call home, these other worlds, that's where I feel safe. Because everything is transparent there. You cannot hide anything. But this has been amazing. I have been taken to a place where my soul has come back with hope. The optimism has come back.*

I just want to say thank you, Rita.

R: Thank you, dear Terry. The pleasure is also mine.

PART 5

Letters from Ketki and Terry Evans

Three letters from Ketki

Life, death and Ray of hope

I had a reasonably happy life, with its fair share of challenges and its rewards. Suddenly and quite unexpectedly, things took a drastic turn into a hitherto unknown direction.

I was newly married, a fresh postgraduate student and possessed with the energy and optimism that comes along with young love and early years of my career. It was during such times that I reconnected with Ray, my childhood friend. I had always admired her, for how literate she was. She was also an articulate orator and a delight as a writer. She could converse in any setting and on any topic.

That one week with her was life changing. On the first day, during our lunch meeting over pizza, we had a conversation on marriage and companionship. She, still a spinster, had said "I want to be married and have someone special in life. Parents, friends, siblings are with you only for a short while in your day. But I want somebody to witness my life up-close. I want some-

body to know how I look early in the morning or in the middle of the night. I want someone to wake up next to me or fall asleep watching me. I want someone to document who I am. I don't want to die single!" We both giggled over this proclamation. The next day, we received the news of the demise of one of our friend's parents. Ray messaged me that night, saying: "Life is so unpredictable. We need to live our moments fully and cherish our time". I agreed wholeheartedly.

The third day, we met and spoke about books and careers. She then said to me: "We are all artists, musicians, dancers, writers. Everything else is just a way to pay the bills". It struck a chord immediately. Ray knew I was known for sports in school. Yet, she didn't include sports in this. Later when I reflected upon it, I realized this had a deeper meaning for me. Artists, musicians, writers, dancers are all expressing themselves. Sports, on the other hand, stems from competition. Even though I had made a name for myself in sports, I did not associate with it, because it was not an expression of who I was.

We then walked towards a newly opened library and Ray just had to check it out, bookworm that she was. I was not such an avid reader, but I enjoyed libraries. She navigated the aisles of books with the expertise of a veteran, all the while commenting on different books we passed by. We finally stopped by the aisle called "Classics". I thought this would be a good place for me to pick a book for myself. So, I asked her opinion. I ran-

domly picked up the nearest book and asked her if she had read it. She said she had. She commented on the author's style of writing and language flow. She refrained from giving any comments on the content. "Go on, read it for yourself," she said. "Okay, I will start with this book, but maybe later," I assured her. This book later turned out to be a key instrument to orchestrate my new life.

By the end of the week, in the middle of the night, I received the news of Ray's sudden death. The world as I knew it, came crashing. I didn't know why, but her loss impacted me in a way I could not fathom. I rushed to her home early in the morning. There I found out that Ray and her brother had both died due to accidental poisoning in their own home. I saw her, one last time, ready to be taken to her final resting place. She looked so much at peace. There was a calmness about the whole atmosphere. Yet, I was filled with rage about how unfair this is. Here is a young, talented and driven person, who had all desires to live and contribute to society. Why did she go away like this? I looked at her parents, who had just lost both their children in one fateful incident. Two accomplished, kind and responsible individuals, gone away too soon.

When I met her mother, she failed to recognize me. She was physically greeting everyone, but mentally, she seemed to be in a different world. I stared into those expressionless eyes and gently touched her, to try to snap her back into reality. I introduced myself to remind her of who I was. Suddenly, there were tears and the eyes now reflected a deep pain, which seemed to come from the soul. She said to me: "Wake her up. Wake my kids up. Ask her to stand up." Her eyes clearly said to me, that her daughter should have been here, with me, like me, excited about the future. My whole childhood flashed before my eyes, memories of us growing up together, eating pizza, writing essays, reciting poems. We had grand ideas to change the world, of women's liberation, of science, of knitting scarves even. Here lay a person, whom I had watched grow and had also grown with. What do I say to her mother? There is nothing that can be said. She is right, her daughter deserves to wake up. How do I make this right? Seems like not even God can fix this!

I plunged into an abyss of grief after this, where everything was meaningless. Life was so unfair that there seemed to be no point or purpose in doing anything. Innocent lives were cut short so mercilessly. I refused to participate in anything that would make me even remotely happy. Until one day, my husband suggested that I join the library, as a distraction. I was suddenly reminded of my visit there with Ray. I went there and picked up the book we had discussed. It was "Many Lives Many Masters" by Dr. Brian Weiss.

I had no idea what the book was about when I picked it up. When reading it, I was introduced to the idea of the soul. After many weeks of pain, I found a release. I slept well that night, *after many nights, finally believing that Ray was okay. I hugged her memories and found comfort, even in death. I took it as a sign that she knew I would need this and hence led me to the book.*

What I didn't know at that point was it being the start of a journey. Six years after her death, Ray guided me again when I once again reached the abyss of grief due to my family situation. I reached a point of seemingly no return. I was reminded of my situation during Ray's demise and sought to read the book by Dr. Weiss again. Only this time, I didn't find it. But while searching for it, I was recommended another book: "Journey of Souls" by Dr. Michael Newton. The book did not solve my problems, but it brought the necessary "Ray" of hope. I was now ready to seek my solution, to ask for help.

I read about the Michael Newton Institute and started looking for a therapist near me. I was disappointed that there wasn't anyone located where I lived. I held on to the faith that when the time is right, I will find the right person to help me on this journey. As fate would have it, the forces conspired to move me from my home in the tropics to the icy Finland. I have questioned this move several times and I am not fully sure what I am doing here. But, it has brought me closer to Sweden, where I met the wonderful Rita.

It has been a few months of association now, and I feel better equipped to handle the grief. I am slowly changing my perspec-

tive and learning who I am as a soul. I am learning to find beauty in everything, including grief and loss. This is not an easy process and no doubt I will fumble a lot. But I believe my guide is around and I will be shown the way, if need be, at the right time.

Sometimes I have failed to see things for what they were. Even though my sister is younger than me, she has often bullied me, without me realizing. I had been conditioned to treat her like my own child (even though she is only 3 years younger) and hence I overlooked the impact she was having on me with her words. Now I seem to notice this better and have begun to object to unfavorable comments. Now I am ready to live life for myself and not be a forced parent to a sibling. I feel like a weight has been lifted off.

Lots of love
Ketki

Dear Rita,

I read the latest draft of your book and it looks wonderful. I think it has shaped up so beautifully. I liked the paraphrased parts, where you have described the essence of the conversation without using the actual dialogues. I think that brings out the context so well.

I always enjoy reading the Leyla story each time you kindly share the draft with me. It is such a simple story with deep meaning. It serves as a good reminder that sometimes the most satisfying life experiences occur within the four walls of your home, with just your family. I always look at Leyla in wonder, how content she was with being a wife and mother and living in the one home for her whole life. She did not feel any need to seek challenges outside the house, to wander and travel or have any other strong purpose outside her family. She also did not feel guilty about her good fortune or question the blessings that came her way. She truly accepted life as it was and experienced divine love in her existence.

In these Corona times, Leyla is a good example to follow. With so many of us being forced to stay indoors for months, we must look for contentment within, rather than outside. During the early days of the pandemic, there was a phase when I expe-

rienced the "survivor's guilt". I constantly felt guilty that I had a job, a house, good health and access to food, while many other people who are equally deserving lost one or more of these. Each time I read of the death of a noble doctor or social worker, this guilt would increase. Then there was news of so many young people losing jobs and plunging into debts, having had their entire lives turned around so badly in just a few days. I felt undeserving of the good fortune coming my way.

Reading this story brought me peace again. It felt like a higher power was giving me permission to enjoy my blessings. I think occasionally, it is a good reminder to enjoy the things that you have, without guilt or worry. I believe your book is coming at a good time, where the world needs these reminders now, more than ever. It encourages us all to look inwards, be content and grateful and be unafraid to enjoy your blessings.

My best wishes to you for getting the book published. May your message reach far and wide.

Lots of love,
Ketki

August 5th, 2020

Dear Rita,

Thank you for sharing the draft of the book with me again. How lovely the forewords are. Dorothea has explained the concepts so well and summarized your story of the book aptly. Both of you are so wise and kind at the same time. I enjoyed reading how she has summarized my part of the story. She got the gist of the session so well. Credit must go to you for this, since you have conveyed the important aspects and retained the essence so precisely.

I am happy to hear that summer is going well. I hope all goes well with the events and lectures as well.

I have had a good summer as well, spending time with my husband and little girl. On the spiritual front, I recently read a nice book called "Purpose". It spoke of purpose of life and purpose in life. The author mentions how the purpose of life is the same for all souls. It is about the evolution and refinement of the soul. But the purpose in life is different for each of us and depends on the "blueprint" that we made for ourselves in the soul world. Many thoughts seemed to align with the key points of Dr. Newton's work, as well.

My personal learning over this season has been about acceptance of our limitations. At times when I witness the struggles of another person, I have often experienced this strong urge to try and make things alright for them. I have tried in the past to make their objectives my own. Now I am learning to set boundaries. I realize that everyone comes with their own blueprints. I must be helpful and kind, but it is not right for me to try to transform somebody's life, just because I believe they will be better off. I must accept that each soul is unique and independent. While we do have influences over each other, our journeys are personal, after all. In someone else's story, I am a bystander, a side character. I must not take center stage there. It is amazing to notice that after each such learning or realization, I find myself to be calmer and happier.

I thank you once again for getting me started on this spiritual path. I am truly enjoying the evolution of my soul, which I have experienced since then.

Lots of love
Ketki

A letter from Terry

Thoughts after the LBL-session

Before the Life between Lives-experience I had with Rita Borenstein I always took my own personal development very seriously. But after that session my mind keeps offering me new realizations that I have not had before. For instance, how I have carried mindsets from previous lifetimes. This has been liberating for me. As those realizations floated up in my consciousness I began to realize the pain, the disappointment and the fear that I brought through to this lifetime. In the first incarnation experience from my life in Germany I was carrying papers that I believe were about research. As far back as I can remember I have always been interested in the mind and how it works. What is the supernatural? What happens in the part of the brain scientists tell us we hardly use? My life was nipped in the bud in that incarnation at the age of 22. This now makes sense. In this lifetime, my journey continued at the age of 22. That was when I had my first consultation with a psychic medium. The same medium told me many years ago that I would be involved in research, which has come to pass.

In the second incarnation that I experienced with Rita, again we returned to Germany. I found myself to be a member of a family and a regime that did not offer anybody a choice. In this lifetime, I am creative and I want to explore and pioneer. I have a feeling that I cannot waste time and to accomplish as much as I can. If I am in a situation that gives me the feeling of imprisonment it is very difficult for me. I remember many years ago a psychologist told me: "Once something becomes an institution and you feel confined, without a voice, you will leave the situation." That can also be tracked back to the incarnation during the Second World War. I now understand why I find any form of dictatorship abhorrent. I was even more inspired when we came to the part where I was being taken into the future. As the realizations floated up into my mind, it was as if I gained control over my fear and resistance. This unconscious fear no longer has control over me, as it did before the meeting with Rita.

Meeting Rita started a whole new process within me. It has given my life new strength, new meaning and hopefully a new direction. The journey that she took me on was amazing. It opened new doors within my mind and it was very interesting how it also helped me clear some mental and physical blocks that I had, but never realized.

After the session, I thought about 40 minutes had passed, but when I checked the clock 4 hours had passed! I thank Rita once again for the gift she gave me.

PART 6

~

Conclusion

~

Let the beauty of what you love be what you do!

Rumi

Conclusion

Sitting in my garden
under the appletree

As a young nurse, I had a longing to go out in the world for a mission of some sort, but did not know what it meant. For many years, I was working in hospitals and health clinics. Although I loved my profession, it left me with a feeling of something missing, especially the older I became.

Now when I am nearly 65, I realize that my whole life has been a constant longing and search for my own soul. Following the lead of something greater than myself seems to have become my inner compass. Step by step I have found what I was looking for. "I was there all along and I was also waiting for you", my soul tells me.

In my work, I witness beautiful moments when people meet with their own soul. In deep trance during their LBL, they also meet their childhood selves, even as early as in their mother's womb. In this early stage of their life and deeply hypnotized, we research their constellations with parents, siblings and family, if possible. What did their soul choose to experience in the environment they were born into? In an LBL-session it is possible to mend old wounds in this life and heal past life traumas. A fragmentation might have happened during many difficult lives and traumatic ways to die, as well. It takes time to heal, but sometimes a quantum leap happens. To have a fundamental and deep healing experience in an LBL, seems possible for those who are ready for it. It does not happen without individual preparation and far from everybody finding their session equally life changing. Those who book a session with me often have a long history of spirituality in one way or another. I cannot take anyone into an awakening which they might not be ready for in their development as a person and as a soul. A session is always a teamwork with the Divine and with trust in the process.

Being an LBL-facilitator is different from being a therapist. When I facilitate the session in an authentic way, the client has their own freedom with the support from me during their process as I advocate for the person's soul. I ask questions and help them get the most out of it. Often my presence and soul essence is like an amplifier or pacifier which facilitates for them to meet with their guides and other helpers in the spirit world.

I have noticed that the interest for LBL has increased during the pandemic in 2020-21. Members of the Michael Newton Institute were given the opportunity to do LBL-sessions online during this time. At first I felt reluctant, but then I experienced many wonderful online sessions, so it seemed to work very well for some, but not all, clients. Those who would have to travel far to have a session with me, suddenly had the opportunity online instead.

Life is a beautiful gift. We are all unique individuals, souls and human beings. The possibility to get to know your soul, to fall in love with it and to remember who you are in the core of your being, is a lovely thing. When we find strength and courage within ourselves deep inside, we have the possibility to grow as human beings. Like with diamonds, the pressure we experience over time makes us stronger, but also hopefully humble and kind.

Thank you!

Ann-Sofie Hammarström Östergren, I am lucky that your talent and long experience as a graphic designer and your skills to make beautiful books have been made available for me by a divine spark.

Ketki, your LBL-session and our correspondence about your story in this book has been a fulfilling and heartwarming experience. Your well written letters add an extra spice to the book.

Terry Evans, your loving kindness and consent to use your fascinating LBL in my book has been a great source of inspiration for me. Your sincere letters in the book add your extraordinary gifts to express your soul in writing.

Dr. Dorothea Fuckert, my LBL and meeting with you in April 2019 was a wonderful healing experience. Thank you for your well written and interesting foreword. Our loving friendship means all the world to me.

Ann-Christine Magnusson, you have been such a great source of inspiration and support for me in my process with this book.

Roger Gotthardsson, to meet a kindled soul like yours in this life is precious to me. Your foreword is a great contribution to my book.

Peter Bodhi Anand Ullberg, your fascinating way to create magic through your presence behind the camera is amazing. The way we met in my garden several times, reflecting on the magic of life, you showing me all your extraordinary cameras that you are constantly schlepping along, gave me magical memories to store in my heart for rainy days.

Further reading

Books by Dr. Michael Newton
Journey of Souls 1994
Destiny of Souls 2002
Life between Lives Hypnotherapy for spiritual regression 2011

Books by The Newton Institute
Memories of Afterlife 2011
Little book of LBL 2018
Wisdom of souls 2019

Michael Newton Institute
www.newtoninstitute.org

Rita Borenstein
www.ritaborenstein.se